coming out
a handbook for men

coming
out
a handbook
for men

orland outland

alyson books
los angeles | new york

© 2000 BY ORLAND OUTLAND. ALL RIGHTS RESERVED.

MANUFACTURED IN THE UNITED STATES OF AMERICA.

THIS TRADE PAPERBACK ORIGINAL IS PUBLISHED BY
ALYSON PUBLICATIONS,
P.O. BOX 4371, LOS ANGELES, CALIFORNIA 90078-4371.
DISTRIBUTION IN THE UNITED KINGDOM BY
TURNAROUND PUBLISHER SERVICES LTD.,
UNIT 3, OLYMPIA TRADING ESTATE, COBURG ROAD, WOOD GREEN,
LONDON N22 6TZ, ENGLAND.

FIRST EDITION: JUNE 2000

00 01 02 03 04 **a**   10 9 8 7 6 5 4 3 2 1

ISBN 1-55583-514-7

LIBRARY OF CONGRESS CATALOGING-IN-PUBLICATION DATA
    OUTLAND, ORLAND.
        COMING OUT / ORLAND OUTLAND.
        ISBN 1-55583-514-7
        1. COMING OUT (SEXUAL ORIENTATION)—UNITED STATES.
    2. GAY MEN—UNITED STATES—LIFE SKILLS GUIDES. I. TITLE.
    HQ76.2.U5 O983 2000
    306.76'62—DC21   00-027274

COVER DESIGN BY PHILIP PIROLO.

For Clint Wyatt,
Partner in Crime,
1965–1994

contents

Introduction

Coming out of the closet as a gay man can be a delightful experience, a frightening process, and sometimes both. By accepting your sexuality and acknowledging it publicly, you are about to enter a whole new world. You are going to make enemies out of people you've never even met, and you are going to make friends with people you probably would never have otherwise met.

Coming out can seem, at first, like jumping without a parachute. When you were a kid and your family moved to a new town, the neighbors organized a "welcome wagon" to fill you in on the good stores, the good schools, and the bad part of town. You quickly met the other kids in the neighborhood, and they told you which house the old witch lived in, where to get the best candy, the best secret places to play, and which teachers to avoid. If you went to college, you were taken in hand and sent through orientation, with a helpful older student showing you your way around the campus.

But when you realize you're gay, it can seem as if you're on your own. Your parents, having had sex together to have you, are probably heterosexual and have no advice to offer you on the world you're about to enter, and there is no orientation program to help you adjust (though there probably ought to be). Chances are you've cobbled together a picture of your future life from an old Damron travel guide you peeked at in the local independent bookstore, the plot of *Dancer From the Dance*, the later episodes of *Ellen*, and the reminiscences of your high school drama teacher. *You are not ready.* But if I've done my job, after you read this book you will be a whole lot closer to ready than you were before.

This book is a substantial update on Alyson Publications' previous book on the subject, *Coming Out Right*. While much of the advice in that book still holds true, substantial changes in the gay community and the straight community's treatment of us have necessitated a whole new book. However, I would be out of line if I didn't acknowledge the previous guidebook on this subject as my jumping-off point.

For the most part this book is geared toward the younger reader. Coming out can happen at any age, though, and there are sections in this book that address the special concerns of men coming out later in life. But in today's relatively liberal climate, it's most likely that a gay man will come to terms with his sexuality earlier in life rather than later. Moreover, the visible gay culture in the big cities is composed of bars and clubs geared toward the young or the worship of youth. And while this is most certainly not all of gay culture, it is the entry portal for most gay people, and it holds its own particular set of hazards for the young gay person, both in terms of physical dangers (sexual diseases, substance abuse) and mental and emotional dangers (the danger of getting caught up in a "bar mentality," in which you measure yourself and everyone around you on the basis of looks, money, and penis size). While a man coming out later in life has lots of lost time to make up for, he's also had the benefit of years to mellow in certain emotional departments and consequently won't face the same hazards younger men face.

This book is divided into two parts. First is an introduction to gay life and some of the challenges you will face during the initial coming-out process. Mostly, this section deals with the above-referenced entry portal to the culture—the gay nightlife. Most gay people's first experience with a large group of other gay people happens in a bar, and there's no reason you should walk into your first gay bar without some idea of what you might find. This section also covers all the aspects of sexuality you will encounter during a surprisingly short amount of time spent in your new community

The second part of this book deals with the world beyond that entry portal, where most gay people end up living and working—the world of community activism, social activities, politics, and just about everything else in the world there is to do besides hit the bars, as well as how to deal with the pitfalls that await you—gay bashers, scam artists, and the police.

So let this book be your welcome wagon, your orientation session, and your friend as you come to terms with the fact that you are a member of a group that is always and forever going to be a minority on this planet and that your life is and always will be, in some ways, different from the life lived by the majority.

part one

Coming Out

Chapter One

Telling Yourself; Telling Others

The first person you have to come out to is yourself. Anyone who has been through this process can tell you that, depending on your circumstances, this can be either the easiest or the hardest part of the whole process. If you are lucky, you come of age in a liberal, tolerant atmosphere, attending a school with other smart, sophisticated young people for whom being thought of as prejudiced is a worse taboo than any difference you could present; perhaps you've had an openly gay teacher, or your parents have openly gay relatives or friends whom you have come to know. In such a case, acknowledging your sexuality is a path that has been smoothed for you.

If you are not lucky, you live in a conservative community where boys still use the word *faggot* as a taunt, you had a gay teacher who everybody knows about but who would sooner die than present his sexuality publicly, or you have parents who profess religious beliefs that are dependent on scapegoats for a sense of personal righteousness (and that set of scapegoats nearly always includes homosexuals). In this case, accepting your own sexuality will be harder, as you will know damn well that being known as gay in such an environment could lead to grief, if not bodily harm or ostracism from your family.

Your first step in either case is going to be to look in the mirror and say to yourself, "I'm gay." No, you don't have to make your first announcement over a public address system like Ellen DeGeneres's character did on the show. Maybe the first time you say it you have to whisper it to yourself in the bathroom, with the door shut, the water running, and the fan on. But whatever the age at which you come out, this has to be the first step. For some gay men it's a knowledge they're born with; for others it's something they repress and deny for years.

No book can tell you how to accept the fact that you are gay. What a book can do is help you after you've accepted that fact, even if that acceptance comes laden with feelings of guilt, shame, and fear. The process of coming out is the process of dealing with those feelings, both in yourself and those around you, and building your self-esteem by standing by your declaration and seeking out those who will congratulate rather than condemn you for choosing not to live a lie.

Coming out will always be scary, but anyone coming out today is more fortunate than his predecessors. Gay people—real gay people, as opposed to the stereotypes foisted on the public in the past—are everywhere in our culture. A gay person does not have to look as far and wide for a "normal" gay role model as he did 20 years ago.

The first thing you have to do as a gay person is learn to screen out the noise, by which I mean, realize that a lot of people are going to denounce you as sinful, sick, or even evil. Yes, there are still people in this country so screwed up that they can't sleep at night for worry about what other people are doing in bed. Don't worry that they hate you; they can't really hate *you* when they don't even know you. People who want power have found that the best way to get it is to frighten people; frightened people naturally herd together for safety and look for a leader. Over the last century power-hungry men have used black people, women who worked, immigrants, single mothers, Planned Parenthood, and all sorts of other groups as a means to frighten their sheep. But as the rest of the country becomes more tolerant, these shepherds are running out of people to hate. In fact, gay people are pretty much the last group left that it's OK to beat on. Always remember when you hear these bigoted individuals speak that it's not about you, it's about them and the tools they use to keep their power base. They want you to feel bad because that helps the people they are using feel better.

Part of screening out the noise is knowing what to expect. There are still popular myths about gay people that will be thrown in your face, and it's best to not only know what they are but also to be armed with responses. Here are the most typical ones:

Gay people are child molesters. Child molesters come in every stripe, but the fact is, most molestation is done by a relative of the child or a close family friend, and even then the perpetrators are quite often married with children. Rarely does a healthy, well-adjusted, out-of-the-closet gay man turn out to be a child molester. Part of the reason this myth is perpetuated is that gay men often refer to other gay men as boys, as in "I picked up this hot boy last week." This almost never refers to actual underage boys and is instead a reflection of many gay men's obsession with youth. It's not unknown to hear a 40-year-old man telling a potential partner "I want to be your boy." In no way does this parlance mean that actual boys are involved.

Gay men are lisping, mincing sissies. It doesn't help a poor gay boy out in the middle of nowhere when the only real gay people he sees (as opposed to TV characters) are the outrageous drag queens the far right culls from footage of San Francisco's yearly gay pride parade. In fact, most gay men wear drag maybe once a year, or maybe once in their lives, just to have what is actually an interesting experience. And some never do it at all. There is no doubt that some gay people are naturally more effeminate than others, but being gay in and of itself is not going to make you a sissy.

Gay people recruit unsuspecting young people into their ranks. This old chestnut is fading away; even the far right knows how silly it sounds.

You can no more "recruit" people to change their sexuality than you could recruit them to change their natural eye color. The fact is, what the Right fears is that gay youth will be exposed to positive gay role models, which will make them more likely to accept their own sexuality. Keeping young gay people away from positive gay role models is crucial to the Right's desire to keep young gay people as miserable and as far in the closet as possible.

If you're gay, you're going to end up with AIDS. This is the lowest scare tactic in the world. All gay men *do not* get HIV. Sick as it is, it's almost as if it pleases some people to think their children and their friends' children will literally die of being gay. The worst part is this is one of those taunts that worms its way under your skin, and once you're out and a member of a gay community, it comes back to haunt you—a feeling of inevitability about catching HIV is a danger under the best of circumstances. As such, the people who say AIDS is inevitable are engaging in the most hurtful behavior possible; sadder still is that some of them actually believe what they say and think they're doing you a favor by warning you. But this is, plain and simple, *a lie.* The only person who can infect you with HIV is you, if you aren't safe.

Homosexuality can be "cured." This is the lie du jour. Recently, right-wing conservatives have paid huge sums of money to run full-page ads in newspapers around the country featuring testimony from "cured" homosexuals who say that if gays and lesbians embrace Christ, they can be converted to heterosexuality. But what these people are doing is not changing their sexuality but suppressing it in order to please others. The whole point of the ads wasn't even to get gay people to try to convert; like everything the far right does, it had political reasons behind it. Americans who have a difficult time with the issues around gay rights often wish, as we all do from time to time about sticky problems, that the issue would just go away. Thus, the Right capitalizes on this by telling *them* the problem would go away if homosexuals would accept the "cure" for their "disease." If a sizable number of Americans can be deterred from acceptance of homosexuals and steered back toward resentment and anger, then the Right will have won a battle in its war for temporal power. If anyone tries to pull this argument on you, just remind them that there's no need to cure something that's not a disease.

Coming out is a process that has changed dramatically; now you even see kids coming out on TV ("Ricki, I'm gay"). But that's like coming out to everyone in your life in a mass mailing. After you accept yourself you need to come out in phases, starting with your friends, moving on to your family, and finally letting the world know. This is what therapists call "building ego strength." You start with the people who are going through the same changes and crises you are going through, and who will be the most sympathetic, then move on to your family, who may have a harder time with it but who, for the most part, will eventually accept it, if not endorse it, and finally you will be ready to live openly in the world as a gay person. Each success prepares you for the next, bigger challenge. Each setback teaches you something you can use in your next coming-out encounter. At the end of the process, you will be a stronger person, having not only forged an identity for yourself but also having fought to have it accepted.

Coming Out to Friends

Each of your friends is going to react to the news in a different way, depending on his upbringing, his sexual insecurities, and his degree of perception and empathy. "I know you are" may be the second-easiest thing you could hear from a friend, the easiest being "So am I!"

"I know you are" may worry you; you might start thinking, *Am I such a flaming queen that* everybody *knows?* Well, if you were, you wouldn't be worried about coming out since everyone would already know—and some gay men adopt flaming mannerisms as a way of coming out without actually having to discuss the subject with friends and family. But close and perceptive friends will have noticed things and figured it out for themselves—the fact you've never had a girlfriend, or if you have, you've never been terribly physical with her; the way you talk just a little too much about or stare just a little too hard at that guy on the wrestling team; the way you freeze like a deer in the headlights when someone tells a gay joke…

The best thing about friends is they are usually sympathetic and are not likely to reject you. And the best way to start coming out is with your best friend, the person who has the most history and connection with you. Even if he has problems grappling with the idea, to him you are probably still going to be a good friend first and a homosexual second. And if he can't handle the news and rejects you, your friendship was built on sand; sooner or later something else would have come along to destroy the relationship.

Your straight female friends are the next group to talk to. Some of them may take it hard, especially any of them who might have a crush on you or whom you might have dated as a "beard." (See the glossary at the back of this book for explanations of new and unfamiliar terms.) They might feel you can be "converted" if you have good sex with a woman, or an ex-girlfriend might feel guilty that she somehow failed and "drove you" into homosexuality—or she might be angry, feeling that you used her to cover your real sexuality. But, all in all, most women are happy to have a gay male friend, someone who can be both a confidante and a window into the world of men.

The stickiest situation is going to be with your straight male friends. They are the ones most likely to feel threatened and become upset. Why this is hasn't been fully figured out by even the best minds, but a lot of it has to do with their own still unresolved sexual identity issues. Homosexuality makes straight men uncomfortable because the idea of it threatens the world of the locker room, the barracks, or any other all-male enclave, often the only places where men feel they can relax and be themselves, show emotion, and let down their guard. If the whole messy arena of sex is suddenly introduced into these environments, it threatens to shatter an already-fragile peace of mind.

Try to understand that prejudice is often fueled less by hate than by fear—in this case fear of things not just outside themselves but potentially inside themselves as well. Your straight male friends have probably taken it for granted that you were "one of them," and suddenly, in the eyes of the society they are so worried about fitting into, you are not. Could the same thing happen to them? They often feel like extraordinary measures need to be taken to make sure that doesn't happen, even if that means cutting a friend off.

Again, you never know—some straight guys have grown up with gay uncles or mom's gay best friend or some other kind of positive message at home about gay people, or they may be so comfortable with their own sexuality that you pose no threat. Moreover, many straight guys are learning that a lot of girls just love a guy who's man enough not to be scared of gays!

Coming Out to Your Family

Again, how easy or how hard this is going to be will depend on your parents' experience with gay people. An accepted gay relative (as opposed to a tolerated relative) or a close gay family friend will make their path toward accepting your homosexuality a little smoother. I wish I could recall where I read the story of the young man who came out to his parents, who looked at each other, sighed, and said, "We thought you'd never figure it out." This is the least likely scenario, of course, but there couldn't possibly be an easier one.

Even if your parents are generally accepting of gay people, it's quite another thing for them to learn that their own child is gay. It's like the movie *Guess Who's Coming to Dinner*—black people are just like us, until one of them dates our daughter. I was lucky with my own parents; my father had worked in Army intelligence during World War II, before the gay purges of the McCarthy era, and a lot of the spies he worked with were gay; they would come over to visit him and cry on his shoulder about some paratrooper they were in love with. My mother's brother was an openly gay man living in San Francisco with his lover, and we visited them all the time when I was growing up in the 1970s. (It was from his turntable that I discovered the joys of ABBA and the Village People.) All the same, when I told my mother I was gay at the age of 21, she said, "Oh, I don't think you are." She knew that all my friends were gay because I'd told her they were. Nonetheless, *denial* is the most common response parents have to the news.

If your parents have a negative reaction to the news, remember that there are many factors at work, most of them societal in nature. They worry what the neighbors will say, what their own parents will say, or that you will be unhappy as a member of a persecuted minority. They will wonder if they somehow failed as parents.

If you are still a minor or still dependent on your parents for support, before coming out to them you need to gauge just how volatile their reaction might be. If your father foams at the mouth at the dinner table every time gay people make it onto the news, you are not a coward if you keep your sexual identity a secret from them, at least until you are financially independent. There are plenty of homeless street kids who are there because their parents instantly disowned them and tossed them out of the house. This is an extremely rare reaction, especially today, but if you think there's a chance of it, hold off. If you are in a situation where you must tell them, say, before another boy's parents have the chance to call them and tell them what the two of you were found doing, try to have a fallback position, a place where you can stay for a few days until things cool down. The best option is a close relative's or friend's house, or you can get in touch with a local gay and lesbian service agency and see what might be available. Such agencies are generally listed in the yellow pages and on Internet search engines under *gay hotline*.

Most parents are going to have some difficulty with your news. This is why you need to build up confidence and ego strength by telling friends first. You might also wish to tell your brothers and sisters, or at least any of them you are close to, before telling your parents. Children are usually at least a little in league together against their parents, and your brother or sister might have a better idea about what your mom and dad's reaction will be, especially if they are older and have already confronted your parents with adult-type problems.

To be a fully healthy individual, you *must* tell your parents eventually, even if you have to wait until you are on your own. But there is no question that the sooner you can tell them without endangering yourself, the better. One of the worst things that can happen to you is to become a closeted gay man, unable to take the next step of coming out in the world, getting to be 30, then 40, then 50, concealing your sexuality, using indefinite pronouns, and avoiding long-term relationships, all because you are still afraid to tell your mother.

Coming Out in the World

Coming out in the world can be far easier emotionally and far harder physically than coming out to loved ones. The people you go to school with or work with or live around are acquaintances, and their opinion of you is never going to matter as much as that of your friends and family, so if they reject you, it's not going to hurt as much emotionally. However, these are also people who don't know much about you before they find out you're gay, and since they don't know your other qualities and have no reason to try to maintain a connection with you as your friends and family do, it is easier for them to reject you, even to hate you.

On the other hand, because they have no stake in you, it can also be easier for them to accept you, or at least regard the news of your homosexuality with apathy. You are stuck with your family for life, but a school or a job can be changed if things get too bad.

Coming out in high school can be painful or relatively painless. It all depends on geography, curriculum, and the state of sexual confusion of the young people around you. Coming out in an Iowa farm town or a predominantly African-American urban high school are experiences more alike than not—both environments are isolated from the wider world, with a predominantly conservative religious outlook and a prevailing macho attitude that will not tolerate queerness. It is necessary for you to come out fully in the world, but sometimes you have to know when to attack and when to retreat. As with a family situation where the news might get you thrown out on the street, don't feel the need to declare yourself in a school or other public situation where doing so might get you beaten up.

Coming out in college is a much easier task. Even the most backwater institution has a way of liberalizing the community it's in, and as the young people in it are exposed to a wider world, and to people not exactly like themselves, they become more tolerant. Moreover, you are going to meet a lot more gay people at college than you did in high school, not only because it's not as necessary to stay closeted anymore but also because gay people are more likely than straight people to take avenues like college that promise an escape from the oppressive environment they've grown up in. Unless you're off to Oral Roberts University, you'll find that most college students pride themselves on open-mindedness. In your new environment tolerance and acceptance are actually virtues, and intolerance and prejudice are actively denounced.

How well your coming out in the workplace will be received will vary wildly and unpredictably, all depending on the personal experiences (if any) of your coworkers and bosses with gay people. The best thing you can do is be good at your job; if you are respected for that when you break the news, it will smooth your path.

Unless you are one of those people immediately identifiable as gay, chances are that your coworkers are going to be mostly unaware of your sexuality until you fill them in. It will not be necessary to do as Scott Thompson did in the Kids in the Hall movie and lead a parade down the street, announcing "I'm gay!" with the chorus echoing "He's gay!" Offices are boring places for the most part, and people make up for this by gossiping about other employees. Once a handful of people know you are gay, everyone will know.

In some work situations it is not advisable to come out. Remember that you are a minority and there are few laws to protect you from discrimination. Even if there were, if a prejudiced boss wants to get rid of you, he will find a way to do it that will stand up in court. If you feel you are in a situation where making your sexuality public will get you canned, keep silent, but look for another job. Nothing will make you more miserable than spending the rest of your life in a job where the only way you can have your boyfriend's picture on your desk is to have him be one person in a group shot, where you will have to either bring a beard to the holiday parties or come alone, where Monday morning will always require you to make up a story about your weekend. That's not a healthy way to live.

When you find a work situation where you can come out, the best way to do this is to display no shame. If someone asks you what you did over the weekend, look him in the eye and say, "My boyfriend and I repainted our apartment," or whatever it was you actually did. Don't waffle and weasel around; if you are going to come out, just do it. If you declare it with no shame, it makes them wonder if maybe it's, well, you know, normal after all. If you blush and use indefinite pronouns, if you are ashamed, it will be easy for them to feel that you ought to be.

"Are You the Man or the Woman?"

When people tell their coming-out stories, they have one thing in common—there is always an amusing (at least in retrospect) moment when someone to whom they have come out asks a question so ignorant it's nearly impossible to laugh. "Why do you want to be a girl?" is typical, as is the question that heads this section. If at all possible, don't laugh. If they ask, they are genuinely curious and are not to blame for having been kept in the dark.

There is no easy way to explain how the dynamics of a gay relationship (especially the sexual dynamics) are different from those of a straight one. To say we are no different may be politically expedient but untrue. We do have different options and conflicts in our relationships, and trying to explain that you can *both* be the man often leads you to discover even more roadblocks in the head of the person asking the question.

The number 1 question you will get will be a two-parter: "Have you ever had sex with a woman? If not, how do you know you won't like it better?" Toss it back, gently, with a smile. "How do you know you might not like *men* (or *women*, if you're talking to one) better if you've never tried it?" In doing this you will discover something the two of you have in common sexually: You both know what you want and don't want.

The details of coming out are different for everybody, but the journey is the same. We start by accepting ourselves, then ask acceptance of our loved ones, then of people we work and live with, and finally, fully comfortable with ourselves and having built a circle of people who love and respect us, we demand acceptance as our human and American right.

Self-acceptance, however, is not something that happens once. For the rest of your life, you are going to be under attack by people who wish you would simply cease to exist, if only because your unwillingness to be herded into a pen you don't belong in threatens their political agenda. These people are like a virus, always finding new ways to undermine your self-confidence and your position in the world. But if you have built that circle of people who love and respect you, you will have the strength to resist such attacks.

Resources

Of all the coming-out stories ever written, Aaron Fricke's *Reflections of a Rock Lobster* is an enduring classic. The true story of a young man who decided to take his boyfriend to the high school prom, way back in 1979, is a great humorous entrée to the world of coming-out stories.

On a darker but still satisfying note, Alan Helms's *Young Man From the Provinces* tells the story of a man who had all a gay man could desire, externally at least, but who failed to achieve self-confidence until later in life. It's about building self-esteem on your own foundations and not someone else's.

Another good read is *Becoming a Man*, Paul Monette's National Book Award–winning autobiography.

There's no better resource for anyone coming out to his parents than Parents, Families and Friends of Lesbians and Gays (libertynet.org/~pflag). The group even has a downloadable brochure on doing it right.

San Francisco's Lavender Youth Recreation and Information Center (thecity.sfsu.edu/~lyric) is one of the best places to go for help or information. No matter what your story, the staff has heard it before and can help.

To find out whether the laws of your state protect you on the job from antigay discrimination, start with the National Gay and Lesbian Task Force's home page (ngltf.org). This is a site that is not going to disappear, and it will have regular updates on the law.

Chapter Two

Your First Gay Social Experience

As a gay man, a great disadvantage you have that other minorities do not is that you are not born and raised with your own kind. The day is coming when "your own kind" will mean the community you grew up in, regardless of your sexuality, but that day is not here yet. You need to meet other gay people for a variety of reasons, the least of which is sex. You need to meet people who understand your experience of growing up gay, who share your sensibilities, and who can help guide you through the experiences you are about to have. If you are lucky, you'll keep most of the friends you had in your pre-out life, and to that group you will add gay friends.

Your first trip to a gay bar is part of losing your "gay virginity." Losing your virginity should be a gentle initiation, and this is true not only of your sexual virginity but also of your social virginity. Your first bar experience will be as memorable as your first sexual experience.

Most gay people are eager to get into their first gay bar, and most of them will find a way to do it whether they are of legal age or not. If you are underage and planning to get into a bar with a fake ID, be prepared for rejection. As far as doormen are concerned, anything that's not a passport or a driver's license from the state you are in is a suspicious piece of identification. If you think you're going to get in with an "international student" ID, don't count on it—these are the most notorious pieces of fake ID in the world. Some bars will take just about any identification that says you're 21, under the assumption that if law enforcement comes looking for underage drinkers, they can always say they saw your ID and it said you were 21. Usually, however, bar owners know that the alcohol bureau isn't going to buy that story, and they won't let you in with a suspicious ID.

If you are in a small town, your options will be limited. There may be only one gay bar, or there may not even be that. In most areas, though, within driving distance you can find a bar where, at the very least, gay people are a part of the crowd, if not the exclusive clientele. Small-town gay bars are usually more wary about admitting young people, as they are more at risk of sanctions at the hands of an outraged populace. Then again, your youth may be so alluring to the other customers that the owner will risk losing his liquor license in exchange for the additional bar take. It won't take you long to find out which way the wind blows in your town.

The winds of progress have brought gay communities to most mid-size cities in America. Even if you live in a small town and can't get your hands on one of the national gay guides from Damron or Ferrari, or even the new line of gay travel books from Fodor's, if you have access to a computer with an Internet account, you are only minutes away from locating your nearest gay community. As of this writing the best starting point for anyone looking for gay and lesbian information on the Net is the book *Gay and Lesbian Online* by Jeff Dawson. The book gives Web addresses for thousands of sites on everything gay or of interest to a significant number of gay people, from the New York City Opera to www.gaysexlive.com. (Yes, *Gay and Lesbian Online* is from the publisher of this book, but it's also a great reference.)

It used to be that there was only one entryway into the gay community: the bars. They were our Ellis Island, the place you were processed on arrival. The Internet has turned Ellis Island into a supersonic airport (aren't we all sick of that information highway?) that allows you to reach any destination—as long as you know where it is. Many of the search engines like Yahoo! support regional categories that include a tab for an area's gay and lesbian community. And many cities have some kind of "gay chamber of commerce" with a Web site listing gay-owned businesses and other attractions popular with the local gay community. The best thing about these community pages is that they give options other than bars. Community Web pages give information on social clubs, political groups, and community-service organizations, as well as bars. If, for whatever reason, you decide you don't want your first gay social experience to be alcohol-related, your best bet is to log onto the Internet and check out one of these many social activities.

If you are underage, gay-youth groups are probably your best bet for meeting gay people your own age. As a gay person who's probably felt isolated and different, your experience with group activities may have left a sour taste in your mouth, but a gay-youth group is a chance to meet other people who've been in exactly the same boat. Most medium-size and larger communities have a gay-youth group.

If you do decide that a bar is where you want to go, it's best to be prepared.

Going Out by Yourself

Ideally, you shouldn't have to go alone to your first gay social spot. If you've come out to friends and they've reacted well, ask one of them to go with you for moral support. If you ask a straight male friend, don't be surprised if he turns you down; it's one thing for him to accept you, quite another to ask him to go into the lion's den. If you have a gay friend, that would be a dream. Otherwise, ask a female friend to accompany you.

Going alone into a new environment is easy for some and tough for others, but it's hard to imagine anyone not being nervous before his first encounter with a group of people who may, by the end of the evening, turn out to be his beloved new tribe, a group of alcoholic sexual predators who sicken him, or anything in between. If you must go alone, and if you have no gay friends or acquaintances to ask about where to go, here are some things to know.

Before you go to a bar, you may be sorely tempted to indulge in a little liquid courage. Don't! In a new situation it's best to have your wits about you. In fact, if you can, try not to drink at all on your first occasion; if you're worried about looking "sissy," order a club soda with a twist so that it looks like you're drinking a cocktail. This first trip is a learning experience, and would you get drunk before going to school?

If you decide to drink, stick with beer, or ask to have your cocktail made with minimal booze (the bartender won't tell anyone you're a lightweight). Many young people have a fondness for sweet alcoholic drinks like rum and Coke. Remember that sugar speeds the absorption of alcohol into your bloodstream, and you will get drunk a lot faster on sugar-laden cocktails than you would on the same amount of booze without the mixer.

If you're going to drink, make sure your wallet is in a safe place and that you're not carrying your life savings in it. Any crowded bar, gay or straight, is an opportunity for the unscrupulous to pick your pocket, especially if they see you're so drunk you wouldn't feel it if they pulled your underwear off, let alone nipped a wallet out of your back pocket. Make sure you bring enough money to get home in a cab, and don't spend it on drinks—even if you find someone to spend the night with, you may find yourself wanting to get out of the situation in a hurry, or he may promise you a ride home later or in the morning, only to end up leaving you to your own devices. In other words, bring what women used to call "mad money."

You should also be aware of the political ramifications of your choice of beverage. For example, many gay establishments don't serve Coors products (this includes Zima) because the Coors family gives a lot of money to right-wing antigay groups. You might get a nasty response from a bartender or angry glares from other patrons if they see you putting a nickel in the pocket of people who are out to make your life, and theirs, a living hell. Don't worry too much, though, because as of this writing Coors is pretty much the only beverage that will get you in trouble.

Bars are pretty much divided into two types—cruising bars and neighborhood bars. Cruising bars are places to dance, hang out with friends, and most of all to find someone and get laid. Neighborhood bars are usually friendlier, smaller, and less likely to result in sex but more likely to result in friendship. Believe me, if you are under the age of 30, you won't have to look hard for sex. But friendship is never as easy as sex, so don't dismiss a neighborhood bar because it feels like "nothing is happening there" when you walk by and look in. Yes, in some of these friendly little bars, you're going to run into some guys who are a little too friendly, a little too fast, but if you are nice in a firm way about rejecting them, even they may end up being your friends—but more on the topic of pickups and rejection later.

Sometimes your best bet is to go into a bar for the first time during off hours. Three o'clock in the afternoon can be a little depressing when you see who's drinking at that hour, but it's still a good time to scope the place out; that way when you come back when the joint is jumping, you won't be entering entirely foreign territory. Most bars are busiest right after work during the week, after 9 o'clock on Friday and Saturday nights, and on Sunday afternoons. Sunday nights are sometimes busier than you might expect, as many people in "gay professions" (like hairdressers and actors) have Mondays off.

A lot of people go to bars looking for sex, but others are just there to drink, to wait for a friend, or to hang out and not be alone. If someone smiles at you, it doesn't necessarily mean he's going to jump your bones, so smile back; it doesn't commit you to anything more. If someone approaches you and hits on you, try to remember that the first person who talks to you doesn't have to be your date for the evening. Talking to someone might lead to sex, but it might lead to friendship, either with him or his friends. It also gives people a chance to observe you in an active, animated state (talking, maybe laughing) rather than a passive state (sitting, drinking, staring into space), and most people are more attractive when animated.

When you're having a conversation with one guy, don't let your eyes wander incessantly around the room looking for someone better. Be polite. If you're not interested in talking to him, excuse yourself to go to the bathroom or to look for a friend. Almost nobody will try to buffalo you into staying and talking, and if that happens, all the more reason to go.

Going Out With Friends

When you go out with friends, a lot of the same rules apply, including not tanking up before going out. However, when you're with a friend, you *can* look around to see what's going on and who might be interested in making eye contact with you. But don't be a teenage girl. "He's looking at you, tee hee hee!" "Is he really? Omigod! Tee hee hee!" If you're in a bar, you're over 21 (or you're supposed to be). So act like it. Don't behave as if you were still in the high school hallway between homeroom and study hall.

Remember, a gay bar is not a theater—don't act. When you're talking to your friends, don't gesture wildly, make big dramatic silent-movie faces, laugh too loud, or do anything to attract attention and make people think you're interesting. At best, they'll think you're nervous; at worst, obnoxious.

Make a pact with your friends before you go out. Don't abandon a friend for a trick, especially on your or his first trip to the bar, or if you're his ride home—even if he says it's OK. He may just not want to sound like a spoilsport, even if it means a grueling ordeal for him to get home on his own. And do I really need to tell you that if you're driving, one of you needs to stay sober to cart the others home?

Getting a Surprise

If you're flying blind, you may find yourself in a bar where you don't feel welcome or comfortable. The rainbow flag outside might lure you in, but then you discover that everyone else in the bar is in heavy leather, or dresses and wigs, and there you are in your Abercrombie & Fitch, feeling out of place. Don't be embarrassed about turning on your heel and walking out—you're not offending anybody by acknowledging that you've walked into a sub-subculture that isn't your cup of tea and backing out gracefully. If you're with friends, don't stand there giggling—just go. You can laugh your head off once you're outside.

Ending the Evening

If you are young, it's probably not going to do any good to suggest that you go home alone or with your friends at the end of your first night out. This is your first chance to do what the grownups do, i.e., find someone and go home with him, and if you are young, you are not going to have to wait long before someone attractive offers you that option.

If you are older, you may be eager to make up for lost time. You have been thinking about being with a man for so long that the idea of waiting another day is almost unthinkable. But the best way to end your first night in a gay bar is to leave alone or with friends.

The reason I'd suggest not leaving with someone for sex is that it makes a blur of the evening, and it puts you in the habit of thinking that going out and socializing with other gay men has to involve ending up in bed with somebody. If there is one serious downside to the way the gay community is structured, it's that the gay ghettos are built around the bars, bathhouses, and sex clubs. Consequently, many gay men learn to relate to each other as sexual objects first, and people second. Do this long and often enough and it becomes the way you relate to every gay man you meet—you end up rejecting people even as friends because they're not someone you're interested in sleeping with.

If you go home with someone your first night out, what happens later may ruin the memory of the whole evening for you. If you find someone you're really attracted to and who's really attracted to you, trade phone numbers—yes, most people never call the numbers they get, but if you were that hot for each other, it'll happen.

The bar, and all the men in it, will still be there tomorrow, and the next day, and the next. If only just once, if only just this first time, go home and to bed alone and think about what you've seen and done. Losing your gay virginity should be a beautiful experience, and it's an experience almost entirely under your control. The first time you go out to play with the other gay grownups can never be repeated. If you end this first experience with a clear head, it'll be a memory you'll never regret.

Chapter Three

Getting Laid

Sex is a wonderful thing. In fact, sex is about the best physical experience you can have, sometimes producing a degree of pleasure illegal in most Southern states. Certainly there are gay men who have no desire to engage in casual sex, but the majority go through, at the very least, a period of experimentation.

A Note for Teens

Many boys, gay and straight, have their first sexual experiences with other boys. There are a lot of reasons for this, foremost for straight boys are proximity, convenience, and the need to "get off." Gay boys, of course, have an additional set of reasons.

For many gay teens their sexual experiences are limited to boys their own age. Once upon a time, such sex meant nothing but pleasure. But today, if you are sexually active as a teenager, even if only with other teenagers, there is a strong possibility you have slept with at least one person who has slept with someone you don't know anything about. In other words, you are at risk for HIV infection if you are having unprotected sex, even with other teenagers. The road to HIV infection is paved with rationalizations, and for young people the most popular rationalization is "I'm too young to get it." Remember, though, that some of your partners may have a thing for more experienced guys who've been around the block a few times or may be shooting up or may have gotten HIV from a blood transfusion. It's never too early to begin practicing safe sex.

Many men have had some kind of sexual experience long before they're old enough to go out looking for it in the gay ghetto. Nonetheless, there are also plenty of people who have *not* had any kind of real sexual experience with another man. So in the interest of being comprehensive, I am going to start at ground zero. If you don't need to start at ground zero, just keep skimming until you arrive at something you don't already know and then start reading. Whatever you do, though, don't skip the information on safe sex.

Safe-Sex Basics

Your first priority should be to have safe sex. Do not kid yourself that you won't get "it" if you have unsafe sex only once or try to convince yourself that if you don't get it the first time you play without a rubber that you're immune. On the other hand, don't let anyone convince you it's inevitable that you'll get HIV—if you play safe, you will almost certainly never get it from sex.

If you're engaged in any kind of sex that involves putting a penis in an orifice, you are putting yourself at some degree of risk of contracting HIV. However, different kinds of sex pose different kinds of risk. Below is a chart outlining degrees of safety for various sexual acts:

Safe:
Mutual masturbation
Frottage (i.e. rubbing your penis against someone's belly, leg, etc.,

or between his legs)
Dry kissing
Oral sex with a condom
Playing with sex toys such as dildos (if you don't share them or if you use a rubber on them and change the rubber before someone else plays with it)

Possibly safe:
Oral sex without a condom
Anal sex with a condom using water-based lubricant (oil-based lubricants can cause the rubber to break)
Fisting with gloves
French kissing

Definitely unsafe:
Anal sex without a condom
Fisting without a glove
Rimming (licking someone's asshole)
Sharing sex toys without using and changing rubbers

The position of oral sex on this list is a controversial subject. There are people who have engaged exclusively in oral sex and contracted HIV. Remember, HIV is transmitted through semen and blood; if you have a slight cut or sore in your mouth and someone who is HIV-positive comes in your mouth, you have an open portal for the virus to enter your system. Generally, however, oral sex without a condom—though by no means *safe*—is considered far safer than anal sex without a condom.

Recently, an idea called "negotiated risk" has gained currency in the gay community. It basically posits that you cannot spend your entire sex life in a plastic bag. For example, the only way to make oral sex completely safe is to do it with a condom, but anyone who's ever had a dick with a rubber on it in his mouth can tell you there is not a whole lot of enjoyment in it. Negotiated risk accepts that life is never completely safe, but it also realizes that you don't do stupid things like walk in front of a speeding truck or get fucked without a rubber and pretend that nothing is going to happen to you as a result.

There is a glossary in the back of the book to explain unfamiliar terms, but two of the words you will hear tossed around when you start meeting men for sex are *bareback* and *raw.* These mean having anal sex without a condom. Inarguably, anal sex without a condom can feel better than anal sex with one, but it doesn't always have to be that way. With the right condom, the right lubricant, and the right partner, protected sex can feel just as good as bareback sex—without the worry afterward about whether or not you just got infected. *Don't let anyone talk you into barebacking.*

Here is a list of the various kinds of protection available:

Latex condoms:

These are the most readily available sources of protection; most drug and convenience stores sell them. Latex condoms vary widely in price, performance, and pleasure. The best condoms are made in environments as well suited to the production of microchips or pharmaceuticals as to rubbers. Such condoms are the least likely to have been exposed to anything that could lead them to break during use. A condom can be cheap and still be reliable but will probably not be that pleasurable. If you are going to stick to safe sex the rest of your life, you cannot consistently use condoms that rob sex of all pleasure, no matter how cheap they are. If money is an issue, you can quite often go to a local AIDS or youth-service agency, or even Planned Parenthood or health clinic and find fishbowls full of mid-price condoms for free. Help yourself; that's what they are there for.

Some latex condoms are lubricated, some are not. Lubricated condoms are lubricated on the outside, and won't slide off your penis during sex. Some condoms have nonoxynol-9, as do some lubricants. This is a spermicide that *helps* protect you against HIV but does not protect you 100% against it. Don't kid yourself into thinking that using lubricant with nonoxynol-9 and no condom is going to protect you. It won't. Some people have a bad reaction to nonoxynol-9 and need condoms and lubricant without it, though this is rare. (Nonoxynol-9 is also a mild anesthetic. It can slightly dampen sensation in your penis, which is something to remember when selecting lubricant for masturbation.) *Latex condoms need to be used with water-based lubricants; oil-based lubricants such as Crisco can cause a latex condom to lose integrity and break during sex.*

Natural or lambskin condoms:

These are condoms made of animal intestine. As an organic substance they are far more pleasurable to both parties, but *they are little defense against HIV.* Biological material is porous. Lambskin condoms are better than no protection at all but only marginally—it takes only one particle of virus to penetrate the condom to infect you. Lambskin condoms are *not* a safe choice.

Polyurethane condoms:

These are a new product, available as of this writing as Avanti condoms under the Durex brand. These are excellent condoms in terms of both protection and comfort, giving both parties a lot more sensation than latex condoms. These new condoms are a lifesaver, literally, for people allergic to latex. Furthermore, polyurethane condoms can be used with oil-based lubricants.

The downside is that right now these condoms are expensive, though that should change as other companies bring them to market and competition brings the price down. For the most sensation with the best protection, these are the ones.

Female condoms:

These condoms, marketed under the Reality brand, were originally designed for women to wear with men who refuse to wear traditional condoms. Informal testing revealed they were ideal for anal sex, giving both parties a higher degree of comfort and pleasure than male condoms, with just as much protection. Of course, our federal government, with homophobic Jesse Helms controlling every appropriations dollar, has decided not to publicize the advantages of female condoms for use in anal sex. Aside from the plastic ring that has to be inserted in the rectum, the only downside to these condoms is the same as with the Avanti: price. However, they are worth a shot; many men who tried them never went back to ordinary rubbers, and men who refused to use protection for erection-related reasons found a way to stay safe and still keep it hard.

Male condoms come in different sizes. If someone tells you his penis is too big for condoms, buy him a box of Maxx condoms. Also, beware of men with small- or average-size penises who insist on using a large condoms (yes, it happens). Oversize condoms are likely to slip off during intercourse, heightening your risk of infection.

Before you go out looking for sex, be prepared. You should have plenty of rubbers and water-based lubricant at your house. Additionally, you should carry at least one rubber and a pocket-size serving of water-based lubricant (available at most sex emporiums). This guarantees that even if you end up at his house and he says, "Damn, I don't have any rubbers," you do. He may just not have been prepared, or it may be a subtle way of introducing the subject of sex without condoms. If you have one with you, you're less likely to be tempted by the alternative.

Losing Your Virginity

If you can, you want to lose your virginity to someone who will care about your pleasure, who may even be turned on in a positive way by the idea of helping you lose it. You don't want to end up with some-one who only wants to "deflower" you because he's run out of other thrills to get him off.

If you are in a situation where you can have gay books around the house, I suggest you pick up a copy of *Gay Sex* by Jack Hart or *The Joy of Gay Sex* by Felice Picano and Charles Silverstein. These are books that contain information on just about everything two men can do with each other, as well as comprehensive safer-sex information. If you can't or don't want to buy or order one of these books through your local bookstore, you can order them over the Internet from a variety of sources.

Otherwise, here is a condensed version of what to expect during your first sexual experience with another man:

What Not to Do

In sex, aside from the rules of safer sex, there is only one thing not to do—don't do anything that doesn't feel good to you. If you are uncomfortable, in pain, or even just bored, you need to speak up. You don't have to say "I don't like that." Instead, you could say "Let's try this," giving a suggestion that will steer the experience away from whatever it is you aren't enjoying. Sex is about giving the other per-son pleasure as well as yourself, but don't think that you will please the other person by doing what he wants when you don't want to do it; for most people at least part of what gets them off is the response they get from their partner. So if you're not enjoying whatever it is you're doing, he probably won't either, unless he's so hell-bent on his own satisfaction that you're more like an orifice than a person—in which case you're better off ending the encounter there and then.

Foreplay

Foreplay can be defined as anything that happens before penetra-tion. The main purpose of foreplay is to find the other person's hot spots. Certain kinds of foreplay can occur in a bar or club before you go home with someone; if you press your crotch against someone's ass and he wriggles with glee, he probably wants you to screw him.

Here's a sampling of things you might want to try, to see what response you get from your partner. Again, if it doesn't excite you both, then move on to something else.

Nipples

For some men their nipples are their G spot. Lick them, brush them with the hairs on the back of your hand, squeeze them lightly, or squeeze them hard, either as he asks you to or as you find out which one works best. For some guys all you have to do is pinch their nipples and they get hard. Unfortunately, some men get so addicted to this that you cannot have sex with them without pinching or turning their nipples all the way through the encounter, which after a while starts to feel less like fun and more like operating heavy machinery or flipping light switches on and off. If you are the one getting your nipples manipulated, it's important to remember that expecting your partner to keep his hands on them at all times is sexually selfish behavior.

Armpits

This may sound gross at first, but many men like to lick armpits, as long as they are free of artificial scents and metallic deodorants. There is something earthy and primitive about the natural smell of fresh underarm sweat (as opposed to the smell of dirty, unwashed pits). For most people deodorant is actually not necessary if they shower daily and wash their pits with antibacterial soap. Keep this in mind if you connect with someone who's into armpits.

Lips

A talent for kissing is the most important sexual talent in the world. More men have been dumped because they were lousy kissers than for any other reason on earth. People can forgive lying, cheating, and stealing faster than they can forgive someone who kisses like a fish. Kissing can't be taught in a book; it's an art form that is learned by doing, through apprenticeship with someone who knows how. But there are some basic things *not* to do that you should be aware of:

Don't stick your tongue in someone's mouth in the opening seconds. Work up to it, dry kiss for a while, then perhaps let your tongue flick past his lips and see what kind of response you get.

Don't open your mouth and plant your lips stiffly against someone else's mouth. Nothing is worse than a fish kisser!

Remember that your lips are muscles; you should use them on another pair of lips (or anywhere else they end up) like fingers on a harp. The biggest penis in the world will get you less dates than a talent for giving truly electrifying kisses.

Buttocks

We are moving much closer to the realm of actual sex, but the best foreplay does lead gracefully into sex. What nipples are to some men, the asshole is to others. A little tickling with the fingers, preferably with some lubricant on them, can excite some men like a dose of Spanish fly. Inserting a finger or two can help to loosen the person about to be screwed and is really the only safe way of feeling flesh on flesh in the rectum—even then, some people discourage it because of the possibility of minor cuts on the fingers. Rimming (licking, kissing, or sticking your tongue up his asshole) is considered high-risk, unsafe behavior. Although there is a relatively low risk in terms of catching HIV, there is high risk in terms of catching intestinal parasites and hepatitis.

Oral Sex

You will be hard-pressed to find any man, gay or straight, who does not enjoy receiving a blow job. Why so many gay men also enjoy *giving* blow jobs is a mystery. Whereas anal sex can provide a world of delicious nerve-ending pleasure-receptor shocks for both parties, the thrills of giving a blow job are mostly psychological. Again, practice makes perfect, but here are some things to remember:

Watch your teeth. If your teeth scratch his penis, you risk exposure to HIV, not to mention turning his groans of pleasure into yelps of pain. Cupping your tongue against your lower front teeth and cupping your lips back around your upper and lower teeth is good protection against biting. Don't worry, with practice, you won't even have to think about it to do it right.

Don't gag yourself. Nothing in the world feels better than having your penis deep-throated, and with practice you will be able to deep-throat almost every penis you meet. (You may have to rearrange yourself and your partner on the bed to accommodate penises with certain curvatures.) However, nothing is worse than having someone throw up on you because he is gagging after trying to deep-throat you. Take it slow and easy. Take as much as you can but remember: If it doesn't fit, don't force it.

When receiving oral sex don't be shy about telling someone what you want. If he's biting you, let him know by saying "Ow! Careful there!" or something else nice but definite. If he's bobbing up and down on the first inch of your penis and you want him to take more, ask. But remember, he might not enjoy sucking and not want to say so—you might want to ask him if you're getting that vibe.

Cut Verses Uncut

Cut and *uncut* refer to whether a penis has been circumcised. (Cut means yes, uncut means no.) Some men love uncircumcised penises, while others avoid them at all costs. An uncircumcised penis is likely to get sweaty at the tip, producing what is referred to in the slang as "cheese," because it can produce a ripe smell and taste. If you are uncircumcised, you

are well-advised to keep this area clean and unscented until
you meet someone who genuinely enjoys the by-products of
negligent hygiene.

Anal Sex

This is something few people are neutral about. Either the whole
subject turns their stomach, or everything else, even the best blow
job, is only foreplay in preparation for it. However much the far right
may say about anal sex being "unnatural," it's hard for anyone who's
had really good anal sex to believe that nature didn't design our
insides with this experience in mind. Women have a button on the
outside called a clitoris, which gives them multiple orgasms; men
have a button on the inside called a prostate, which gives them
orgasms. Anyone who can push those buttons the right way will
never be lonely for long.

Chapter Four

Going Out

You might think it would be better to talk about going out and finding someone to have sex with first and then about how to actually do it. But the fact is, most guys are going to have their first sexual experience by accident rather than by design, possibly before they ever go out looking for it.

Later on in this book I'll address the wide variety of social opportunities available to you outside of the sexual subculture, but right now we're assuming you are horny and bored and ready to have some fun.

Getting Comfortable in a Bar

Going to a bar by yourself to meet men is a far different experience than going with friends. When you're with friends you may be more courageous as far as exchanging interested glances and friendly nods with strangers than you would be on your own, yet less courageous about going up to a man and introducing yourself. Being with friends gives you a feeling of security when "cruising" (scanning other guys to see who's interesting and interested), yet it can impede you when it's time to make a move since, if you fail, you are not just rejected but rejected while your friends are watching.

Furthermore, a man you're cruising is more likely to be friendly and introduce himself if you are alone—it's one thing to introduce yourself to someone, another to introduce yourself to someone and all his friends.

If you are really interested in meeting someone for sex, or maybe just for a make-out session, it is often easier to do it on your own than with friends.

When you walk into a bar by yourself, you are going to be cruised. The previous edition of this book hit it on the head: "As you come through the door, some men will probably turn and look at you. Then they will turn away again. You have not been snubbed or rejected: You've just been inspected." Once you are settled in with your first beverage, you will find yourself inspecting the men who arrive after you.

Most bartenders are friendly; in some bars they are notoriously flirty. If the bartender is sullen, I'd advise you to try another bar— a sullen bartender means either a sullen crowd or that you're not welcome. It's a good idea to tip bartenders. In gay bars, if your change for one drink is 75 cents, leave it as a tip. If your change is less, leave a dollar bill. This is based on your basic big-city price for a beer—between $2.25 and $4.50 depending on the establishment. The better dressed your bartender is and the more expensive your drinks are, the more you need to tip. Tipping guarantees decent service as the night wears on. Gay bars can get crowded, especially late in the evening. When this is the case, if you haven't tipped or have tipped poorly, you'll find it difficult to purchase a drink.

A note of warning: Don't fall in love with the bartender. Yes, he is handsome. Yes, he is friendly. But remember, part of his job is to look good and be nice. You are one of hundreds of men he is going to smile at and speak to, so take his friendliness with a grain of salt. As boyfriend material he is better suited for someone who works the same strange hours. Some bartenders are clean and sober (or at least not raging drunks), but the bar scene is full of opportunities for a handsome guy to get free drinks, free drugs, and free love, and most gay bartenders go through a phase where they partake of all that. If you have a chance at going home with a bartender, it will be because he invites you to stay after closing and wait for him. If that doesn't happen, focus your attention on other men in the bar.

Bars are usually set up to allow patrons to be either public or private. If you need a minute to compose yourself, you can almost always find a dark corner where you can sit out of sight, adjust to the environment, and relax. After you (and your eyes) adjust, you can look around and see what's doing. Of course, if you are a social animal who's never had a problem meeting people, you can plop yourself at the bar and immediately start chatting up the bartender and the men around you.

Many bars have two bathrooms by city ordinance, one for men and one for women, even though there may never be a single woman in the place, and if there were, she wouldn't pee there if her bladder were exploding. In some bars the men's bathroom is for peeing and the women's, with its stalls, is for doing drugs. In others you might have one bathroom with only a trough and another bathroom that is locked, for which you have to get the key from the bartender (another reason to tip well). In this case the bathroom is often used for either doing drugs or having sex. Unless you are unusually brazen, you will probably only ever pee while at a gay bar. You are well-advised to take care of "other business" before you leave home.

Most bars have either a dance floor or a pool table. Dancing and playing pool are good ways to meet new people, to put yourself where you can been seen by more that just a few people, and to do something other than stand around and drink. On a busy night, to play pool you'll have to sign up on a blackboard near the table and wait for your turn. When your name comes up you will play the winner of the last game. The new player—you, in this case—pays for the game, so make sure you have the right number of quarters. If you win, you stay on the table and the next guy pays. Don't sign up and then disappear, as the players find it unpleasant to have to shout your name again and again when it's your turn, only to have you fail to respond. If you do miss your turn—because you were sucking face with someone, had to pee, or just didn't hear your name above the noise—don't argue. Just put your name back at the bottom of the list. You'll do better in terms of making friends and meeting potential bedmates by being a good sport than by complaining, even if you were "wronged."

When you dance or play pool you will be exposed to public view, since watching people dance and play pool is what the people who aren't dancing or playing pool do to keep themselves occupied. Don't worry that you're not a hotshot dancer or player; as long as you don't knock anyone over or send balls flying off the table, you'll be all right.

The Opening Gambit

Different men have different ways of cruising. Some simply stare like they're trying to drill a hole in you with their eyes. Some wait until you walk past and murmur a low, sexy "Woof," followed by a grin when they've gotten your attention. And yet others stare at you with their "twin whirlpools of need" and exclaim drunkenly how hot you are and then try to paw you. Try to be polite to anybody cruising you except the guy who paws you—unless you think he's attractive. (The people who grab at you before saying hello are rarely the ones you will find attractive.)

The most polite way to cruise is with a smile and a nod. If you get a smile and a nod from someone, it's OK to approach him. Conversely, if you smile and nod at someone, it's OK for him to talk to you.

The first thing you can say to anyone is "Hi." It gets a little more difficult after that, but the best way to break the ice is to offer a compliment. After all, you approached him (or smiled to indicate he could approach you) because there was something about him that attracted you. You aren't losing any ground by telling him what it is. If you're afraid of embarrassing him, or yourself, you can always give a neutral compliment such as "That's a great jacket."

Everybody knows the line "Come here often?" is a cliché, but it gets used because it's hard to figure out what questions to ask a person you don't know. In a big city the best way to start a conversation is to ask him if he lives in town. On any Friday or Saturday night, a healthy percentage of people in a big city gay bar are usually from out of town.

After that, the conversation will either get rolling on its own or die of its own accord. He might turn out to have interests that coincide with your own, or he might have the pecs of doom and a voice so queeny it makes Richard Simmons sound like Barbara Jordan (a surprise known as see Tarzan, hear Jane). Good excuses to get away from a man you're not interested in are:

"Well, I'm going to walk around, see if any of my friends are here tonight."

"Well, I've got to go to the bathroom; I'll see you later."

"Well, it's been nice meeting you. Have fun tonight."

Don't tell him you're going to get another drink; this is an opening for him to either offer to buy you one or, worse, to ask you to get him one too. Conversely, if you like him and you want to continue the conversation, you can say, "I'm going to get another drink. Can I get you something?"

The First Move

At some point physical contact will ensue, usually a hand squeezing your bicep or shoulder or placed fleetingly on your leg—an indication of sexual interest that falls short of manhandling. Further contact will depend on how attracted you are to each other, how loose your inhibitions are, and the code of conduct of the bar.

A good general rule: the more plants in the bar, the less appropriate it is to engage in heavy petting and face sucking; the more leather jackets in the bar, the more acceptable it is to engage in overtly sexual behavior. Some bars have strict policies, sometimes because of worries about the local authorities, other times because the regular clientele prefers a more relaxed, well-mannered environment.

Making out with someone doesn't mean you have to go home with him. Use your best judgment in these situations. You know perfectly well that if you're French-kissing someone and fondling his crotch, it is way past time for you to tell him you have a lover and that you will be going home alone tonight. There is flirting, and then there is teasing. Of course, you have the right to change your mind about having sex with someone, but if you get to second base more than once in the same bar and then call it off, you will develop a loathsome reputation.

The most inexcusable behavior is to get wrapped up with someone, make out with him, and then ditch him for someone "better" you met on your way to the bathroom. Treating people like cuts of meat will not only be bad for your karma, but it will also eventually ensure that you end up treated like a piece of meat yourself.

We are all nervous and eager to please around someone new and attractive. You may find yourself getting physically intimate with someone just because you don't know how to discourage his actions. Also, making out with someone is often easier than making conversation, even more so when hormones are raging. If you find that someone is getting a little too fresh, say politely but firmly, "Please, I hardly know you!" or, "Sorry, but I don't like to put on a show in public."

Finding Out What You Want to Know

Casual conversation can provide a lot of information but maybe not all you want to know. When fishing for information try to keep personal questions vague, such as "What do you do?" rather than, "Where do you work?" If you are too direct, you might scare him off. After all, you are still a stranger, and more than one of us has been at least lightly stalked by someone who got a little too much personal information a little too soon. Conversely, beware of giving too much information about yourself.

"Do you live alone?" is a good question. Many people with room-mates have agreements about bringing people home. Also, you don't want to go to his place only to have his jealous lover come home and make a scene, or worse.

"What part of town do you live in?" is also a good question to ask before you agree to go home with someone. People may promise you a ride home and then be "too tired" later to deliver. Or they might choose to leave you to your own devices for any number of other reasons. Remember the part of this book about carrying mad money? If you're not getting there in your own car, make sure you've got cash enough for cab fare home.

Ironically, though it might be too personal to ask someone what company he works for, you should feel free, if you are thinking about going home with him, to ask questions about what he likes in bed. After all, his idea of a good time might be sucking your toes for an hour while you stare at the ceiling and yawn.

Part of the gay cruising uniform used to be a colored hankie in one back pocket or the other. While the glory days of the hankie code has waned, there are still a lot of men who wear "flags" to advertise their sex act preferences. A detailed presentation of the hankie code and other flags appears in appendix 2 of this book, and it's a good idea to peruse it before hitting the bars. Also, if someone is wearing a hankie in his back pocket, feel free to ask what it means. You won't be thought ignorant, as even in the glory days of hankies, there were so damn many colors that nobody could remember them all.

Key chains and cock rings are still popular flags, and a lot clearer than hankies. If a man has a set of keys dangling from his left side, or a cock ring hanging off the left epaulet of his leather jacket, he is flagging that he is a "top" looking for someone to please him as a "bottom," usually by sucking him or getting fucked by him. Flagging right indicates you are willing to please a top. Key chains and cock rings are often "accessorized" with a hankie for further clarification.

If your prospective partner isn't advertising his intentions through some form of flagging, the best way to broach the subject of sexual preferences is to ask, "What do you like to do?" He may be vague and say, "Everything." He may be flirty and say, "Anything you want, baby." Or he may be quite specific and say, "I like to get fucked" or something equally direct. Whatever his answer, you'll are likely to come away with a sense of the information you were looking for. If not, feel free to tell him what you like.

Time to Go

Eventually, you and your potential partner have to make a decision: Are you going home together, going your separate ways, or trading phone numbers to get together for a date?

When it comes time to make this decision, the best advice I can offer is to use your best judgment. If there is any question, err on the side of caution. *Be careful out there* is a good watchword. Someone who's a little too jumpy and nervous, whose eyes are a little too wild, may just be a little fucked up on drugs, or he may be a crazy person. He may not kill you and put your head in his refrigerator, but he might rob you or become a stalker.

You have been consistently lied to by your elders about drugs and alcohol, but one thing they told you is true: Drugs and alcohol impair your judgment. Alcohol loosens your inhibitions. And drugs like ecstasy, special K, GHB, and crystal meth—all popular in gay crowds—can make you so horny you don't care if a guy is Genghis Khan as long as he gives you a good lay. It helps to know at least one person in the bar before you leave so that you can drag your date for the evening over and say goodbye. That way your date knows that someone who knows you has seen his face, and if anything happens to you, he will know whom to look for. It's a little paranoid, but it's also a good idea.

If you go home with someone—I'll say it again—have condoms and mad money on you. And don't let him drive you home if he's drunk; insist on taking a cab.

Sometimes you don't go home with someone, but trade phone numbers instead. Sometimes you do go home with someone, have a good time, and trade phone numbers, hoping to get together again. Don't put too many expectations on the call. He may never call, or you may call him only to have him never call you back. Why men do this is a mystery. Some guys do it because they're afraid of how much they like you and that you won't like them as much. Some guys do it because they don't want to get into a relationship with you when there might be someone just a little better for them to meet next weekend, but only if they don't make plans with you. And some guys do it because they're jerks. Don't let yourself get too wrapped up in a fantasy of a future with someone who just walked out the door. If he calls, great; you've got a shot at developing something—a romance, a friendship. If he doesn't call, screw him; he isn't worth the grief.

Chapter Five

Drugs

"Do you like to party?" When someone asks you this question in the context of a sexual overture, he isn't asking if you're a social creature. He's asking you if you use drugs, probably referring to "sex drugs" like crystal meth.

For the most part gay men take drugs for the same reasons anybody else does—to blot out unhappiness, to make sex more intense, to acquire a temporary self-confidence, or to have the energy to dance all night. But gay men have done more "research" than their straight counterparts into the uses of drugs in sexual situations. Once you begin going out to gay venues like bars, dance clubs, and possibly sex clubs, you'll find yourself being propositioned not only sexually but also chemically. The purpose of this chapter is to make you aware of just what you are being offered and the long- and short-term consequences of accepting such an offer.

We have all witnessed the war on drugs, and we have all been relentlessly and shamelessly lied to about drugs: "Heather C. tried marijuana one day; soon she was smoking crack!" (A condensed version of an actual *Reader's Digest* article from 1997.) We are told that studies "prove" marijuana is a gateway drug, meaning that if you smoke pot, you will soon be smoking crack. In researching this book I discovered at least one search engine that responded to *any* query about illegal drugs by bringing up a banner for an antidrug group that read, SMOKE-

POTRYCOKEVENTUALLYDOHEROINEVERYDAY. If this were true, almost the entire population of San Francisco would be junkies by now.

The purpose of this chapter is to give you some straight-up information on drugs, especially the ones you will run into in the gay community. (Alcohol isn't covered because almost everybody has had experience with alcohol and knows firsthand the consequences of excess consumption, and our culture has provided us with pretty straightforward, truthful information about alcoholism.) By discussing drugs in this book, I am not advocating their use; I am giving information about an aspect of gay culture that you are likely to encounter.

I have classified the drugs that will be discussed in this chapter into three categories: 1) marijuana, an intoxicant like alcohol; 2) psychoactive and sex-enhancing drugs, which pose a danger but which people have used recreationally for years without serious side effects; and 3) "heavy" drugs, regular use of which will eventually do just what the drug warriors say—destroy your life.

All drugs do have one thing in common: They alter your consciousness. They make you happier or sadder or just plain discombobulated. It is important to remember that *you are at higher risk for engaging in unsafe sexual behavior when your consciousness is altered.* The problem with substances that make you feel good is that they lead you to want to feel even better, and for many people that means sex without a condom. While your consciousness is altered, it is also easier to convince yourself that it can't hurt to fuck without a rubber "just this once" or that that fucking without a rubber will feel so good it will be "worth it." When your consciousness returns to normal, you will regret your decision and wonder how the hell you could have ever thought that. When you make decisions about drugs, remember that people often do things on drugs they would never do off them.

Marijuana

In a rational society marijuana would be treated like alcohol—it would be legally available, illegal to sell to minors, its sale would be regulated and taxed, and treatment would be available for users who become abusers. Empirical evidence suggests that marijuana is far less toxic than either alcohol or tobacco, but no scientific evidence has been presented to support that assumption. The reports that do come out state that marijuana causes everything from lung cancer to irreversible brain damage. However, many well-informed people feel these studies should not be taken seriously because they are almost always initiated with the goal of furthering the antidrug agenda.

Today's marijuana is not your hippie parents' marijuana. In the plants grown today, thanks to agricultural techniques like crossbreeding and hydroponic farming, the concentration of THC (the psychoactive chemical in marijuana that gets you high) is far higher than it ever was in the '60s. It is possible to find marijuana so strong that one bowl (the amount packed into a pipe) could actually keep a person stoned for days, smoking only a hit or two a day.

In some big cities, especially San Francisco, where there is a highly pro-pot culture, you can find gay bars where pot smoking is not only allowed but is also the reason many of the customers are there. These are almost always bars with outdoor patios, especially in California, where smoking of any kind is prohibited inside bars. It's in these environments that marijuana is put to its best use, that of social lubricant. If you are standing near a group of guys who are getting stoned, chances are that they will offer you the pipe. It's a courtesy, and it's also a good way to introduce yourself to meet people. Marijuana is most enjoyable when smoked with others, whether at a bar, a party, or with friends at home.

Marijuana can make for excellent sex, not only because it can enhance physical sensation but also because it can lower your inhibitions, as alcohol does, without the side effects of alcohol such as impotence, nausea, and a general lack of awareness of who the hell you're with and what the hell you're doing.

If you are going to use marijuana, however, remember that it affects your judgment and motor functions. Do not operate heavy machinery after smoking it—this includes driving a car.

Marijuana is not physically addictive, but it can be psychologically addictive. It can be much easier to assuage loneliness by firing up a joint than by going out and trying to meet new people. Many people who function normally at their jobs use marijuana the way their parents used alcohol—as something to come home to every night to blot out the pain or loneliness or depression. If you aren't careful, you can find yourself living in the pleasant, fluffy world that marijuana offers as a substitute for real life, real people, and real experiences.

Marijuana use (or any regular drug use for that matter) begun at an early age can stunt emotional development. If you are blotting out your more painful feelings with drugs, you won't work through those emotions and find the root causes. In a rational world, therapists would prescribe marijuana to people who have been through emotional traumas to provide an emotional cushion the way other, more physically addictive sedatives are prescribed now.

For people with eating disorders marijuana can be an enabler. THC causes a chemical imbalance that leads to low blood sugar and triggers the munchies, a desire for snacks and especially sweets. The drug blocks signals to the brain from the stomach indicating fullness, so it is possible to gorge yourself when stoned in a manner not possible when sober. Anyone looking for an excuse to overeat is encouraged to smoke marijuana on a daily basis. In other words, if you're on a diet, smoking pot is a bad idea.

Used wisely, marijuana is the best mood-enhancing drug available, legal or illegal. Used improperly, you can find yourself alone in your room for the rest of your life with your TV and your bowl, never knowing what you're missing in the real world.

The Psychoactives

Marijuana is, of course, a psychoactive drug. In its stronger variations it is possible to visit many planets without leaving your comfy chair. But as a general rule, marijuana leaves you "nicely toasted" and is a drug that for many people is best done in mellow environments like their own home.

What we're looking at in this section are the psychoactive party drugs, usually associated with raves or other ecstatic communal events. These include ecstasy, acid, and mushrooms.

Ecstasy

By far the most popular psychoactive drug at this time, Ecstasy (also known as E, X, and buying a vowel), is an amphetamine and hallucinogen that causes feelings of delirious joy, love for one's fellow man, a heightened sensitivity to touch, taste, and sound, and boundless energy.

Ecstasy is methylenedioxymethamphetamine, or MDMA, which is the chemical heir to MDA, the most popular gay party drug of the '70s (after cocaine). Any drug you buy can vary in quality, but X is notorious, especially on the West Coast, for the irregularity of its effects. A hit of X may cost you $20 and keep you in love with the world and everyone on the dance floor for 12 hours, or it may cost you $30 and leave you feeling sore, achy, and speedy.

X should not be taken with alcohol because alcohol diminishes the high and because both substances are dehydrating. The greatest risk from good X is that you can find yourself dancing or having sex for hours, sweating profusely, completely unaware of your dehydrated state. Anyone taking X should accompany it with large quantities of water throughout the high.

People on the anti-HIV drugs known as protease inhibitors, or PIs, need to be especially careful around X because X and PIs can interact dangerously. PIs tend to raise the level of certain drugs in the blood and prevent their metabolism in the liver. Consequently, a hit of X for someone on Norvir can be like ten hits—a lethal dose—for someone not on Norvir. Valium also interacts dangerously with X. In general, you should be aware that *X can and often does interact dangerously with other drugs.*

Ecstasy can be a fun high—if the quality is good and you take it with people you trust and enjoy being around and who will keep you drinking water and prevent you from wandering into the street to dance with the cars. X is an extremely boring drug to take alone.

The reports of people dying from X are not all drug-war propaganda. Occasionally, the manufacturing process creates toxic substances like paramethamphetamine. Bad X can be laced with anything from crystal meth to strychnine. If you are going to do X, it is definitely not something to buy from someone you don't know and from whom your friends have never bought before. There is much rah-rah lore about the drug's role in transforming society, remaking the Aquarian Age for the new generation of love, blah, blah, blah, but the truth is that many a rave scene has been destroyed by unscrupulous dealers who gradually decreased the amount of MDMA in their hits and increased the amount of crystal meth (which is far less expensive). Anywhere there is money to be made, somebody will be ripping somebody off, no matter how many holographic peace symbols bedeck the fliers for the event. If you want to do X, be as sure as you can be that you are doing the real thing.

LSD

Acid is not one of the most popular drugs in the gay subculture. It is a highly potent hallucinogen that does not usually make the user feel like being around large groups of people. People often drop acid at parties, bars where they are comfortable, or at home with friends or a sex partner. LSD (lysergic acid diethylamide) is one of those drugs whose effects cannot be predicted, as it has a different effect on every person who takes it. You might find yourself having horrifying visions of a childhood experience you had blocked out and be unable to stop screaming, or you might spend an entire afternoon lying on a hillside, watching the clouds roll by, feeling a peace of mind you thought unobtainable.

LSD is a drug you should *never* take when you are alone. You are also better off not mixing it with any other drugs, including alcohol or marijuana, as there is simply no telling how it will alter your high.

Mushrooms
"Magic" mushrooms like psilocybin and psilocin are another hallucinogen available on the gay scene, mostly where younger, hipper people congregate. Mushrooms are eaten or brewed in tea— and usually vomited back up not long after the hallucinogenic effects begin, as they cause extreme nausea. The effects often include "hearing colors" or "seeing sounds."

Like LSD, it is important that you not take mushrooms by yourself. First off, unscrupulous dealers have been known to lace magic mushrooms with LSD or even PCP (a.k.a. angel dust, a drug that was briefly popular until it became apparent that many people who took it became completely psychotic while on it).

Sex Drugs

Drugs like X, acid, and pot can be used to enhance sexual pleasure, but sexual enhancement is not their primary use. Most people take X to dance and to socialize, acid to watch the fluffy clouds, and pot to relax. The drugs discussed below are differ from marijuana and psychoactives in that they are most commonly used in the gay community to fuel sex.

GHB
GHB (also known as G and easy lay) is a clear liquid that tastes, at best, like seawater. A central nervous system depressant, GHB (gamma hydroxy butyrate) is sometimes taken on top of stimulants like crystal meth to alter the high. During sex it produces an out-of-body sensation that decreases inhibi-

tions. GHB is also taken in clubs as a substitute for X, though it doesn't produce the feelings of joy or heightened sensory perception of X.

The maximum amount of GHB you should ever take is one teaspoon, the equivalent of one full cap off a plastic soda bottle. *GHB should never be taken with alcohol because this can result in coma or death; more than one dose of GHB within an eight-hour period can do the same thing if you have not built up a tolerance.* The stories of people overdosing on GHB and either dying or going into comas are not antidrug hysteria; the emergency room at San Francisco General sees at least a dozen GHB overdoses every weekend.

As stated before, one of the slang terms for GHB is easy lay. If you are with someone who offers you GHB, be aware that if you take it, you might find yourself engaging in sexual acts you would not otherwise engage in—with him or maybe with anyone.

GHB tastes horrible. If it is slipped into your drink, you will probably know it. If you are at a bar and your beverage suddenly tastes like dreck, or someone gets you a drink and it doesn't taste the way it's supposed to, toss it out and get another, and keep your hands and eye on the new glass at all times. (This is also a good way to guard yourself against Rohypnol, also known as roofies, and the date rape drug, though roofies are uncommon in the gay community.)

Ketamine

Like PCP, Ketamine (also known as K and special K) is an animal tranquilizer and can have the same drastic and not always sane effects. Special K comes in a liquid form that is dried so that the powder can be snorted or remixed with water and injected intramuscularly.

A K-hole, a common effect of special K, is a waking blackout that can last for hours, during which the user experiences a loss of time and even his sense of identity. Ketamine was withdrawn from use as a surgical anesthetic for humans because patients tended to exhibit violent behavior when they regained consciousness.

As an anesthetic, special K can lead you to perform sex acts you wouldn't otherwise perform. You may find yourself being fisted for the first time and feeling no pain and think it is because you are relaxed and ready, when in reality your membranes and muscles are being violently torn up and you just can't feel it because the drug is blocking the pain.

Some enthusiasts compare special K to X as a "social high," though even they admit it's a lousy sex drug. While it is the purpose of this chapter to inform and not command, I would strongly recommend anybody considering taking either GHB or special K to wait until they have seen someone overdose on GHB or fall into a K-hole. Neither is a pretty sight, and both will likely discourage you from trying these drugs.

Crystal methamphetamine

If there is one drug that is predominant in gay life other than marijuana, it's crystal methamphetamine (also known as meth, crystal meth, and crystal). As one user put it, "I've had two experiences in my life that have brought me together with people both above and below my station in life, people with whom I would have never otherwise associated: being in ACT UP and doing meth." For those insecure in the company of other gay men, meth provides a surge of confidence and energy—at least during a user's initial flirtation with the drug. For men for whom one-night stands and casual sex are the rule rather than the exception, sex on meth can produce intense, instant emotional and physical connections with another person. Crystal meth is cheap, around $40 for a bag that will last one person all weekend (at least to start, when tolerance is low), and it is readily available in almost any bar with a reputation for dark-corner nastiness.

For years meth was seen as the drug of choice for so-called white trash—the kind of people who couldn't afford cocaine, the kind of people who were always getting busted on *Cops*. Now meth is widely used by individuals of all classes, especially in the gay community.

If you are in a big city, sooner or later you will be offered meth by a sex partner, a friend, or someone in a bar or club who just doesn't want to be high alone. My opinion is that each person reacts to drugs in a different way. There are people who have used cocaine or crack or meth once and been unmoved, while others have taken one of these drugs and found "the answer"—a state of mind and body that is irresistible no matter how drastically the habit strains the pocketbook or the immune system.

Crystal meth stimulates dopamine production in the brain, at the same time blocking dopamine reuptake. It mimics adrenaline, producing a surge of mental well-being coupled with boundless physical energy. Crystal meth turns sex from a brief encounter into a frenzied lust that lasts for hours, even though both parties often get crystal dick, a complete inability to get an erection. The introduction of the prescription drug Viagra has produced a renewal of enthusiasm for crystal meth sex, as it can not only cancel out crystal dick but also give the user an erection stiffer than anything he could get even when off crystal.

Anecdotal evidence seems to indicate that people get hooked on either crystal meth or cocaine; it's almost as if each brain is wired to love one or the other but not both. People who have used cocaine in the past should be wary about using crystal meth, as they have gotten used to or even addicted to the rush rather than the high. They are used to the short-term effects of cocaine. Crystal meth, however, can stay in your system and be reactivated for up to three days by something as seemingly mild as a cup of coffee.

Crashing on crystal can be a severe thing, especially if you have been on the drug and awake for several days. At a certain point your body will demand sleep, regardless of how much more drug you put into it. Another downside to crashing is that you have temporarily exhausted your natural reserve of dopamine and at least temporarily fried your dopamine-manufacturing center. In other words, *many people experience a severe depression when coming down off crystal meth.* The people most attracted to the drug are clinically depressed individuals for whom it provides feelings of joy not otherwise available; unfortunately, these same people are most in jeopardy of committing suicide or some other dramatically negative act when the drug wears off and they find themselves ten times more depressed than they were before they took the drug—and the only solution is to do ever more meth to ward off depression. Over time, the body and brain adjust to meth, turning the user into an addict. Without the drug, addicts are fatigued and depressed; restoring natural dopamine production (which some say may not be possible) and regaining natural energy levels after getting off the drug can take years.

Friendship and Drugs

There is one sure casualty when you embark on a serious relationship with a hard drug, and that is your relationship with people. The more you are attached to a drug, the less important people will be to you. You will begin by blowing friends off to score or use drugs, canceling plans you made earlier in the week for Sunday brunch because you were out all night Saturday and couldn't possibly sit still, without sunglasses, on a sunny outdoor patio for more than five minutes.

Some of your new "drug friends" might turn out to be lifelong friends, but for the most part they will be people who are, like you, in love with the drug and who will always put it ahead of you. If you lend money to people on hard drugs, do not expect to see it returned. If you make plans with someone on hard drugs, do not expect those plans to come to fruition. If you come to depend on someone to score drugs for you, don't be surprised if you find yourself calling that person only when you want something. And should you ever go into selling drugs, be prepared to spend your time in that profession completely unable to trust any other human being.

Sex on Drugs

Sex on drugs, especially X and crystal meth, can be an amazingly intense experience, leading you to believe that you have found true love. A bottom on crystal meth can get fucked for hours on end, experiencing a continuous state of physical ecstasy. After the fog clears, however, he may suddenly think, *Oh, my God, I can't believe I even did it with him let alone gave him my number...*

If you are going to use hard drugs and have sex, be prepared for this experience. Intimacy and intensity are illusions cast by drugs like X and meth. If you're going to mess with these drugs, remember, it's not you, it's the drugs. It is entirely possible to spend eight drug-soaked hours having sex with someone and use up all the passion you could ever feel with that person over a lifetime.

In Conclusion

You are entering a subculture with a long history of experimentation with new forms of pleasure, including drugs. Be careful. If you are planning to try drugs, try to walk a middle path, where you conduct your experiments but don't become a walking social problem. The major problem with hard drugs is that most people who are highly attracted to them after the first use become chronic users—if not outright addicts. (If you are taking a drug every day, you are an addict. There is no getting around that fact.)

There are plenty of people addicted to hard drugs who nevertheless function. You've heard the term *functional alcoholics*? It applies to other drug users as well. Such individuals have a habit they cannot shake that impedes their social lives, their romantic lives, their retirement plans, their vacation plans, and everything else that makes up a balanced life, but they manage to work well enough to keep the money coming in to pay for the habit. It is possible that you could become one of these people.

Nobody can tell you not to try drugs. Just remember that although there are substances that seem to solve your problems, those substances will present you with a whole new set of problems: how to pay for your habit, how to keep the friends you had before you met the drug, and, eventually, how to face the world without the drug. (You don't see old drug addicts; this is because sooner or later they either die or have to dry out.)

If you have elected to not use drugs at all, I congratulate you. Still, you will have to deal with your friends and their experiments with drugs. You may find it necessary to cut off some friends because their drug use has gotten out of control and they are dragging you with them on their downward spiral, draining you financially and emotionally. You may take a draconian approach and cut off anybody who even experiments with drugs, although to be honest, that will probably leave you a lonely person. The hardest and also best thing you can do when you see a friend become overpowered by his relationship with a drug is to not judge, offering your emotional (not financial) support and trying to provide him with alternatives to the life he is pursuing.

In the end, the cure for a drug problem is not interdiction or punishment or "Just say no!" It's providing people with opportunities to do things other than drugs that make them feel productive, self-confident, and happy.

Chapter Six

Sex—Here, There, Everywhere

Bars are the first and most obvious place to go to meet men, but once you are settled in your new community, you will find others. Just how many and how wild these places will be depends on the community in which you live. In San Francisco, where I used to live, every alternative discussed in this chapter is available, although you have to go across the bay to find a bathhouse. If you live in a smaller or more conservative community, not every option will be available.

There are advantages and disadvantages to these alternative places to find sex. At a bar you are required to make conversation, superficial as it may be, before going home with someone. In most sex club environments, however, you can share an orgasm before you've shared names—if you ever do share names. This ultracasual approach to sex indisputably turns it into a less intimate act, which can lead you to use sex as anything from a hobby, something to do when bored, or as a compulsive pursuit, in which you are desperately trying to score points by proving how many men you can do it with. It would be nice to tell everyone to avoid these kinds of encounters and settle down with someone with whom you will have satisfying sex, but most of us spend at least some time single, dissatisfied, and horny. With luck, you will use these venues as stopgaps and not as a way of life.

Love on the Wires

Thanks to modern technology, you can get laid without ever leaving your house. (This has been possible for years, but we will discuss calling escorts in another chapter.)

Phone sex

Phone-sex lines have been around for many years. Get a gay paper or porn magazine, call an advertised 900 or 976 number and, for a charge ranging from a $2 flat rate for 24 hours up to $2 a minute, you can "talk live with other hot guys in your area." Originally you were thrown into what is called a room with whomever else was calling and said "Hello" to announce yourself, quite often to a stony silence—even though the room was full. With luck, you would talk briefly with someone to find out where he lived and what he was looking for. If you were interested, you'd exchange phone numbers so that you could talk more privately. Of course, after you gave your phone number, you'd find your phone ringing with offers from other people in the room who had written down your number, even though they hadn't said a word while you were there. More than one man has had to screen his calls for days afterward to avoid such pests.

Advances in technology have made today's phone sex more sophisticated, offering private hookups, personal ads, and more. Nonetheless, it has been my experience that phone lines are the most disappointing, most time-wasting, most cost-ineffective way of meeting men. I have encountered more people on phone lines who lied comprehensively about their statistics in the hope that I would go through with sex with them simply because I'd traveled across town in anticipation of what they'd advertised; more people who made dates and sent me to addresses that did not exist; more people who were, in short, liars, game players, dissemblers, or messed up on drugs to the point of severe malfunction than anywhere else in the gay community. I would actively encourage anyone looking for sex to use phone lines only as a last option.

Computer sex

Computer sex has replaced phone sex to a great degree. America Online is the most popular electronic locale for sex, though it is often criticized for censoring content. In another chapter I'll talk about Internet Relay Chat, but that is a less sexual gathering place.

As I learned while writing a chapter on online encounters for my book *The Principles: The Gay Man's Guide to Finding and Keeping Mr. Right*, there is little point in going into specifics about how to use or cruise with a piece of software, as the difference in lead times between updates of books and updates of computer programs is so drastic that any specifics I could give would be out of date by the time the book was published. However, some basics have remained in place in the structure of AOL and will probably not change.

AOL has chat rooms where you can meet other people with similar interests. These rooms are divided into two groups, public rooms featuring groups like Friends of Bill W. and such, and member rooms, where the sex happens. M4M, or men for men, is the code word to look for in member room names if you want to meet gay men. The tenor of these rooms varies wildly. The San Francisco M4M rooms (there can be as many as five at one time) are basically pickup joints; few people join in the room's group discussion (quite often there isn't one), preferring to communicate privately with men whose profiles interest them. On the other hand, Rhode Island M4M is a gathering place not unlike a friendly neighborhood bar where everybody knows each other, mostly because the sexual climate in Rhode Island is not the same as it is in San Francisco. The physical climate also comes into play. Killer snowstorms can leave everyone, including gay men, isolated for days at a time. In such cases, telecommunication may be the only way to get together with other people.

Once you have an AOL account, you will need three things to begin cruising. First, you need a play name, a screen name other than your real name, as you don't want to share you real name with strangers, some of whom are (I speak from experience) sophisticated con men. This could be something like Lookn4it or any other suggestive name of up to 10 characters in length (as of this writing). Your play name should suggest what you are looking for, as this will attract the people you want to meet. For instance, PutItInMe gives a pretty good idea what that person wants.

The second thing you need is a profile. Your profile is a bio that all other members can read. AOL offers you a set of fields with tags like *hobbies* and *computers used,* but don't be shy about ignoring these tags completely and using the fields to fill in your stats, sexual preferences, or anything else you want to share with potential dates. When you first get onto AOL, you might want to read some other members' profiles first to get an idea of what yours should say. But be advised that without a profile of your own, few people will talk to you. This is something people usually do for their own protection, even though a profile can be full of lies.

The third thing you will need is a picture (or several pictures) of yourself, head included. The pictures need to be scanned into a GIF or JPEG format. (Most copy centers can do this for you.) Along with the profile, the picture is the great advantage of computer cruising over phone cruising—you get to read something about the people, get a sense of what they're looking for, and, most importantly when looking for sex, you get to see what they look like. Of course, nothing stops some people from using pictures of other people as their own or using pictures of themselves that are, to be kind, outdated.

A note: AOL does scan profiles for offensive language. The presence in a profile of words like *fuck* will get the profile deleted; the use of similar language in a screen name will result in a terms of service violation notice, which can lead to your entire account, straight names, play names, and all, being canceled. Many unscrupulous spammers—*spam* is slang for electronic junk mail—use *terms of service* in their subject lines to get you to open their bullshit messages, but it is worth opening such messages just in case. Once you realize a message is spam, you can easily delete it.

On AOL you open lines of communication with someone by sending them an instant message, or IM. It can be as reticent as

"Hi" or as forward as "I read your profile, sounds like we'd click, check out my profile, and IM me back if you're interested." Someone may, of course, do the same to you.

There are a wealth of tips to be offered on cruising online, but this isn't the place. You now have enough information to get started, and you will learn the rest from experience. Remember, as with phone lines, you are dealing with people you cannot see, and it is always advisable to take everything someone tells you online with a grain of salt. Someone may slightly exaggerate his dick size online, or he may concoct a life story or even a gender that is not "his" own. Compulsive liars are inordinately attracted to online services because the anonymity of such environments offers them such a wide berth.

Bathhouses and Sex Clubs

In the novel *Fear of Flying*, Erica Jong coined the phrase *the zipless fuck*. She shocked straight America with the notion that a woman might want a casual, anonymous sexual encounter. But gay America didn't blink. Gay men had been having anonymous sex for years, not as bored housewives out looking for a thrill but as frightened men living in a society that gave them no other alternative. Gay sex was done in secret, quickly, each participant fearing the other would expose him.

Much of today's gay sexual underworld owes its existence to this legacy, although each generation of gay men has worked hard to make sex a more positive and less guilt-ridden experience. Bathhouses are the natural result of two convergent forces—the tradition of gay sex as something done furtively in a dark place, and the later, polar opposite view of gay sex as something to have as much of as possible.

Many cities closed the baths after the beginning of AIDS, but others did not, figuring correctly that men were going to have sex and that it was best to ensure they had it in an environment in which they would have access to safe-sex information and free condoms. Those cities that did close the baths, which were quite often places with showers, clean bathrooms, communal spaces, and sometimes even fountains, pools, and gardens, found that they were replaced overnight by sex clubs, usually gloomy warehouses chopped up by partitions, with no showers, filthy bathrooms, and a renewed sense of gay sex as dirty.

Bathhouses and sex clubs are usually public spaces, meaning you will find little, if any, privacy. For the most part this is because monitoring has become a big issue in terms of how municipal health authorities regulate such establishments. Monitoring means that employees are able to cruise the facility, see what people are doing, and stop them if they are not using a condom. Most baths and sex clubs have strict rules about safe sex that are enforced both for your safety and theirs, as the last thing you want is to contract HIV, and the last thing the club wants is to be featured in a local news sweeps-week exposé on unsafe sex.

All bathhouses and many sex clubs expect you to undress when you arrive. You will be given a clean towel, though you can choose to walk around in underwear, a jockstrap, or even nude if you've got the confidence. The basic rule is, no street clothes. You arrive at either establishment and find a window or a desk where you check in. It may be necessary to buy a membership; this is partially to legally protect the owners as operators of a "private club" and partially to line the club owner's pockets. You will be asked for identification; sometimes married men, who make up a significant part of bathhouse and sex-club clientele, turn around and leave at that point, afraid to leave any record of their visit. ID is required to make sure you are 18. In some places your ID is also used as collateral to ensure that you bring back your room or locker key.

Don't go to a bath or sex club where you aren't able to check your valuables. At the baths you are usually offered a lockbox where you must put your ID and membership and where you can also put your wallet, keys, and other small valuables. Sex clubs will often check your coat and valuables in a locked closet.

Baths usually offer either a room or a locker, usually for the same amount of time. Lockers are cheaper, but if you meet someone who also has a locker, you may find yourself at a loss for a place to connect with him. Rooms are small and usually have a mattress on a built-in wooden platform. Some rooms have TVs programmed to show porn videos. Most rooms are completely private—if you close the door—but there is no avoiding the occasional pervert who drills a hole with his key in the thin wall between his room and yours. You might want to check for this before settling into your room; the management will usually give you a different room if you find this problem and object.

Most people go to baths and sex clubs alone, though some show up with friends, often after a night of clubbing or barhopping. If you and your friends are not in the mood to split up when the opportunity for sex comes along, you shouldn't go. The last thing other patrons want is a gaggle of gawkers tittering. It's one thing to chat up friends you run into, quite another to make a night out of ruining other peoples' experiences.

Cruising at baths and sex clubs is a more direct process than cruising at a bar or dance club. At a bar, cruising is an invitation to say hello; at a sex club it's an invitation to grab some ass and go for it. Some people will make eye contact several times before making a move, just to make sure you are receptive. As in a bar, a nod and a smile sends a clear signal of interest and approachability.

If you are looking at someone, whether in the hall, a room, or the showers, and he is not looking back at you after a few seconds, it is not because he hasn't seen you but because he has seen you out of the corner of his eye and decided he is not interested, for whatever reason. Accept this rejection gracefully. (You will likely reject men in the same fashion.) He may not be attracted to Asian men, or he may be attracted only to Asian men, and chasing him around the building showing your interest is not going to increase his.

If someone is molesting you, stand up for yourself. You have to accept that in such a sexually charged environment there will be the occasional brush from an unwelcome hand, but if someone is mashing you, or keeps coming into your room and touching you after you've let him know you're not interested, inform the manager—he wants to know, as people like that are bad for business, and chances are good that if he's doing it to you, he's also doing it to others.

Drug use is much more prevalent at baths and sex clubs than at bars for two reasons. First, baths and sex clubs are usually open all night, giving people on drugs somewhere to go when the bars close. Second, for those on the kinds of drugs that put the sex drive into overdrive, sex clubs offer an endless supply of new partners.

Patronage at sex clubs usually peaks right around the time the local bars close, and attendance remains high for about an hour after that— men who haven't scored at the bar stop in for one last chance at a pick-up or for a quick orgasm before going home alone. After that the major-ity of patrons are as high as a kite. If you are visibly high, be prepared to be asked for drugs. Some of the people who ask may want to have a good time with you, which they would like to see chemically supplemented, but others will hang around only for as long as it takes to get high.

The X-rated Bookstore

For men in extremely isolated areas, an X-rated bookstore with a 25-cent "arcade" is sometimes the only place to meet men for sex. In big cities these bookstores offer a low-budget alternative to baths and sex clubs. In a city like San Francisco, bookstores on Folsom Street are action-packed sex centers for men who either get off on the trashiness of the experience or who just find it conveniently close to the South of Market bars, where-as bookstores in the Polk Street area are basically places where hustlers can pick up and do clients or drugs out of sight of the police.

Some people are extremely turned on by the sleaziness of the arcades, but for the most part they are just depressing and dirty and should be used as a last resort when looking for sex.

Public Sex

In the last few years in the gay community, a whole movement has grown up around public sex, usually referring to sex in nature—at a park or a beach or even in a back alley. Sex in nature can be a galvaniz-ing experience: you, him, the breeze in the trees, the waves lapping at the beach… It is partly thrilling because it usually takes place where the possibility of being arrested still exists, even in sexually liberal climates.

Most large parks in urban locales have an area known for gay sexual encounters. Again, most of these areas are legacies of a time when gay men had nowhere else to meet. But they thrive today thanks to a mix of those who enjoy the danger, those who genuinely love sex in nature, and those who cannot afford to pay a cover charge for indoor sex. The police are not tolerant of these high-shrubbed promenades in parks, although there are some parks that are already disreputable or dangerous enough that a little gay sex takes a backseat, usually to the homeless encampments and drug dealers, in the eyes of law enforcement.

If this sort of milieu is really your thing, just be careful, not only of the police but also of young thugs who go to these parks, especially late at night, precisely to prey on gay men, either to rob them or beat them up or both. Remember that many of the other "patrons" are closeted gay men who are there because it is a place to have completely anonymous sex, and who, when the screaming starts, will run in the opposite direction rather than provide assistance. If you are going to cruise a park, pick one with other activity going on, even if that consists of disreputable people hanging out, as other activity diminishes the likelihood of your being attacked.

On the Street

You are walking down the street and all of a sudden there *he* is— everything you've ever wanted. And he's looking back at you the same way. The two of you pass each other, transfixed. You turn around to see if he's also turned around, and he has. You both stop, smile, and introduce yourselves. Next thing you know...

There is no hard and fast rule for what to do when someone you meet like this. Just use your instincts. Maybe it's one of those magic moments; maybe not. Maybe he's your next husband, or maybe he's been high as a kite for days, walking the streets picking up everyone he can. You'll figure it out soon enough. Remember, though, sometimes the best things come when you're not even looking for them. A meeting like this is one of those adventures that is part of life in your new world. Don't expect it on a constant basis, but when it comes along, and it feels right, enjoy it.

Chapter Seven

The Sex Industry

If you are young or extremely good-looking, or if you have an impressive-size penis, it is possible that someone will offer you money for sex—or to pose nude or be in an X-rated movie. And regardless of your age, looks, or penis size, some night you may find yourself lonely, bored, or horny (or all three) and you might rent a gay-porn video or consider paying somebody for sex. This chapter examines both the buying and selling ends of the sex industry. It does not, however, cover street hustling, as street hustling is not really sex work; it's an act of desperation usually performed by kids with no other alternative, many of whom are not gay. (Advice for gay kids forced out of their homes appears later in this book. For now, though, I'll just say that no number of Gus Van Sant movies will ever turn peddling your ass on the street into a romantic adventure.)

Escorts

Turn to the back pages of a gay community newspaper such as San Francisco's *Bay Area Reporter* or New York City's *HX* and you will find a surprisingly large number of men offering themselves for rent. You may think about the guys in the ads and decide you'd like to try one of them, or you may decide that some of them aren't any hotter than you and that you would like to become one of them.

Hiring an escort

Hiring an escort is relatively easy. Both freelancers and agencies advertise in local gay papers and gay magazines. The first step is to decide what you want. Do you like slim young-looking guys, or big hairy muscle men? Do you want to fuck or be fucked? Do you want to go out or stay in?

Most escorts provide the essential information, except for price, in their ads. The going rate in big cities is $100 to $150. Some escorts will emphasize that their fee is per hour, and when they do so they mean it. Others will give you as much time as necessary. Escort ads feature a code not quite as ornate as the hankie code but still plenty mysterious to the uninitiated. If the ad includes the words *24 hours,* it means the escort is not averse to your being on drugs and that he may welcome an offer of some for himself. The words *uninhibited* and *open to most scenes* usually mean a willingness to have sex without a condom. If the ad says *safe,* it means the escort will use condoms and should not be propositioned for unsafe sex. Most escorts are a year or two (or more) older than what they advertise.

If you have a special request, ask for it on the phone, not when the escort arrives or you may find yourself disappointed when he turns it down.

You are usually better off answering a picture ad than a text-only ad because you can see what you're getting in the picture ad. If you answer a text ad and the man who arrives at your door isn't what was advertised, don't be afraid to call him on it and send him packing. On the other hand, if he *is* what you want but you get cold feet and don't want to go through with it, you really ought to pay him anyway.

Becoming an escort

People turn to sex work for a variety of reasons. Some men become escorts because they want sex all the time and can find at least something sexually attractive in any person they are with, so they put their permanent hard-ons to profitable use. Some men do it because they were sexually abused as children and their psyche is so screwed up that the approval they get from being paid for sex is essential to their emotional well-being. Some do it because they've been laid off from work, have been offered money a hundred times before and turned it down, are sick of the corporate world, or want the life experience, the dinner-party stories, and the under-the-table income the job will provide. Other men do it because the easy money enables them to work one or two hours a day and spend the rest of their time doing whatever they feel like doing. I've known artists who have hustled just enough to pay the bills, leaving themselves free to do creative work without the strain and drain of a regimented job, and I've known drug addicts who have hustled to pay for their habits. There are any number of other reasons.

If you are considering becoming a sex worker, you need to consider how entering this profession will change your life. It sounds dramatic, but the fact is, *sex work is risky business— legally, socially, economically. It is a danger to your health and your self-esteem.*

If you are considering sex work, the first question to ask is, "Do you have to get fucked up to do it with a client? Do you have to have a couple drinks, a bump, a hit?" Anybody who needs to get fucked up to go to work needs to find another line of work.

The second question you should ask is, "Do you care what people think of you?" Most people, even gay people, look down on hustlers. If you become a sex worker, you will have to deal with a large helping of contempt from a large portion of the population. If you do not want to deal with such disdain, then don't become a sex worker.

The third question to ask is, "How well do you handle money?" Most escorts are young men, and most young men don't have the skills or experience to manage their incomes. When a fresh-faced young man goes from making $5.35 an hour at the card shop to $100 an hour tax-free as an escort, the money becomes slightly unreal and tends to flow out just as quickly as it flows in. And when a young man's hustling days are over, there is usually nothing left. Even worse, sex workers have no health insurance, disability insurance, or unemployment plan. If an escort contracts a social disease or even just the flu and doesn't have cash to pay the doctor—most hustlers don't save for a rainy day—he is in trouble. For this reason, if you do decide to become a sex worker, a safe-deposit box with at least several months worth of bare-minimum funds is a good idea. (You cannot deposit your earnings in a checking account without exciting the interest of tax-collecting authorities.)

Another consideration is that becoming a sex worker can ruin your romantic and personal sex life. Most men don't want to date someone who is having sex with other people on a daily basis, and even if you do meet someone more tolerant, you need to think about what your occupation is doing to your sense of intimacy. In other words, when most of the sex you have is work, all of the sex you have can *feel* like work. Some escorts get around this by exclusively being the top with their clients, saving the bottom role for home fun. Even then the job can make intimacy more difficult than it already is. It can be hard work fulfilling the physical and emotional needs of strangers all day, leaving you with very little for your loved one at home.

If you do decide to become an escort, you are faced with two possibilities—putting an ad in the paper or working for an agency. (Some men work exclusively online, with screen names like Il4ku4cash. This is still a rarity but becoming more common as technology advances.)

If you place an ad in the local paper, you've got a choice of a basic print ad or a picture ad. Picture ads are more expensive, but many people call picture ads exclusively as they are often the only ones for which "what you see is what you get." Many unscrupulous people run print ads the way they run personal ads—in short, they lie about vital statistics. *Do not give your home phone number in an ad*. Instead, get a pager, preferably a voice-mail pager so that customers can hear your voice. When you get a message, call back the number he leaves and talk to him. If you are suspicious that he is not aboveboard, call again a few minutes later; if he answers, say you're "just leaving the house." This is a good protection against bullshit calls.

Your ad should contain your vital statistics. Be accurate about your height, weight, penis size, and body type. Like people who place personal ads, most escorts shave a year or more off their age, so if you say you're 24, most people will assume you're 26. Thus, age is a category in which it is almost essential to lie because everyone will think you are anyway. Be specific about what you will and won't do, such as "100% top; 100% safe." Some escorts do in calls, where people come to their house or apartment, but out only calls are the better policy. Otherwise, any kook can easily stalk you.

Have a phone spiel ready. When you talk to someone he's probably going to be a bit nervous. Rehash your statistics, elaborate a bit (you might have to keep it short in the print ad to save money), and ask him what he's looking to do. Try to get specifics so that you are not put in a compromising position once you're there.

You shouldn't have to ask for the money; a discreet person will put it out in plain view so that you can see it when you arrive and you can discreetly palm it on your way out. If your instincts tell you the person is sketchy or too nervous, ask to see the money. Almost nobody will try to get out of paying at the end of the hour if you've already seen the cash in their possession.

Agencies sometimes specialize in a certain type—18 years old or as near as they can get, Asian men, bodybuilders, etc. If you fit a particular or in-demand type, you would probably get more work through an agency than on your own. Most big-name gay-porn stars who double as escorts (in other words, most big-name gay-porn stars) work through agencies. Agencies charge about double what freelancers charge, so their clientele is richer, more sophisticated, and more demanding. To work at one of the better agencies, you must be fit, handsome, and well-hung. You should also be personable, intelligent, and capable of carrying on or even running a conversation with the client, or possibly even his friends at a dinner or party.

The upside of working for an agency is that the people who call are a lot less sketchy than some of the people who call print ads direct. It is far from unknown for someone to call your print ad and send you to a nonexistent address or try to persuade you once you've arrived to do something you clearly stated on the phone that you won't do. But, for the most part, people who call agencies are not shy about stating what they want and having the agency fulfill their desires off a checklist. The agency may also tell the client flat out that any sex that occurs must be safe sex, though for the most part discretion on their end of the phone precludes them from discussing this in great detail. *All our models are safe* is the usual code phrase. A good agency also screens out the freaks on both ends of the transaction, making it safer for both the escort and the customer. The escort usually takes home two thirds of what the agency charges the client.

Massage

Many papers divide their ads between escort and massage ads, though the line between the two is quite blurry. Many people just want to be visited and touched, and massage offers this at a lower price than escorting. The process for hiring a masseur is the same as for hiring an escort, though most masseurs—at least the ones advertising in the gay press—do not work through an agency.

Real masseurs are often listed as certified massage therapists, or CMTs. Masseurs are more likely to show their face in their ads than are their escort counterparts. Many of the ads specifically say *nonsexual,* and if they do, they usually mean it, although some "nonsexual" masseurs will make that decision when they see you in the flesh.

Anybody can run a massage ad, but if you are interested in doing this type of work, you are better off becoming a CMT. Many gay men have made a good living for years doing massage, especially in large metropolitan areas. As a general rule, if you are being hired as a masseur, that is usually what the customer is looking for. Do not be offended if he sprouts a hard-on during the session; you are, after all, touching him in a relatively intimate fashion. You are under no obligation to do anything about his response. You can even ignore it if you wanted to, though it would be more professional to take away his embarrassment by noting that you must be doing something right.

Stripping

Most big cities have an all-male theater featuring poorly projected videos, sticky floors, and strippers. Customers usually pay a cover charge for entry. Once inside they can "tip" the dancers. How much contact is allowed between customers and dancers depends on the establishment. If you are unsure, it is best to follow the lead of other customers. Sometimes the dancers are hustlers. Other times, not. If you want to make a date with a dancer, the best way is to ask him directly, albeit discreetly. If he is available, he'll say so. If he says no, though, he means it.

If you are interested in becoming a stripper, there are a few things that you should know. Stripping is generally considered a sleazy occupation, and you will be looked down on for doing it. In a few clubs the pay is good and the tips are better; in most, however, the dancers are hustlers who work there only so that they can hang out after their show and make dates, which is how they earn their real money. Like modeling for a magazine, stripping can be a way of making money without actually having to have sex with people (if you don't combine it with hustling), although you should be prepared for groping and occasional mauling while performing. A good club will have a bouncer at the ready to take care of anyone who crosses the line drawn either by the club or local ordinance.

Getting Busted

Most police departments tend not to bother with agencies or escorts working through the paper, preferring to spend their resources cracking down on street hooking. All the same, every now and then a blue nose gets out of joint and a get-tough policy is momentarily adopted. A good escort agency will bail out and may even cover the legal bills of its employees. Customers, however, are on their own. Whether you are a seller or a buyer, you should always consider the fact that sex for pay is illegal and can get you arrested.

Modeling

In the classifieds of most gay publications, you will find ads saying something like "Models wanted by professional photographer." Some of these ads are legitimate, especially if they have the name of the photographer or his business in the ad. Others are merely a ruse to get attractive and gullible young men to take their clothes off, with the camera sometimes around only as a prop and the "photographer" tearing his clothes off seconds after the model does.

The magazine racks in gay bookstores are stuffed with gay porn magazines, and it is true that these publications are always looking for fresh meat. If you really want to be in a magazine, you are best off having a friend who is not completely incompetent with a camera take some nude shots of you. You can send them to a magazine that features your "type." If the magazine is interested, the editor will name a price and set you up with a photographer who works for them regularly. Don't expect to get rich, however; the top magazines pay cover models about $1,000 for a set of photos.

For the most part appearing in a magazine is not difficult, and it can boost your sexual popularity. But be prepared for the fact that many closeted gay people in your office or community get their only sexual thrills via the magazines, and as hypocrisy always walks hand in hand with self-repression, many of them will treat you in the manner written about in the section on working as an escort. Being in a skin mag is a declaration of many things—in addition to showing your every attribute, it also means you are 100% out of the closet and prepared for literally anybody and everybody you ever knew to see you nude.

Videos

Gay-porn videos can be rented at almost any independent video store located in a gay neighborhood. Chain stores, even in gay neighborhoods, are far less likely to carry them. Most gay men rent porn movies at least occasionally. No one will look down on you for renting one. If you do not live near a store that stocks gay videos, you can purchase them through ads that appear in most gay magazines or off the Internet. The cost for recently made gay videos ranges from about $50 to $150, depending on the subject matter depicted. Almost any fetish you can think of has at least a few videos available.

Appearing in a porn movie is something that will change your life far more drastically than any other form of sex work. It is not only you naked, but it is also you having sex—for all to see, for all time. If you do an X-rated movie, abandon all hope of a political career.

As with modeling for a magazine, if you want to appear in a video, you are best off sending nude pictures of yourself to a large gay-porn studio. The studios are always looking for a fresh face and will contact you if they are interested. (Smaller porn outfits often do only fetish or specialty films and find their models either by word of mouth or through ads run in gay papers.)

All of the major studios depict safe sex in their films; no anal penetration occurs without a condom. Most of the big studios have a "house" look that they market; Falcon stars, for instance, are usually lean and chiseled, well-hung, and in their early to mid 20s, whereas Titan Media stars are muscular, hairy chested, and closer to 30 or even 40.

Don't expect to get rich by appearing in a porn video. The pay at major studios runs about $500 for each scene you are in. In addition, if you are from out of town, studios will usually fly you into San Francisco or Los Angeles (or wherever it is they are filming) and put you up in a hotel.

Drug use on the set varies wildly from studio to studio and director to director, but you are expected to show up sober at any shoot; if they offer to tank you up, then you are not entirely responsible if you can't perform.

Should you find yourself making a name in porn, be prepared to be despised, envied, chased after, stalked, harassed, worshiped, taunted, cried over, and always, always for the rest of your life stared at and whispered about.

Getting Out

Even someone who works in the sex industry for years, managing to keep a level head the whole time, eventually needs to retire. Everybody reaches a point where he just can't screw one more stranger for money—sometimes sex-work veterans find themselves losing all interest in sex. If you become involved in the sex industry, if you are lucky, you will get out when it feels right, and you will have something positive to show for it—the ideal being a set of good memories and some money saved up.

For many people, though, sex work becomes a trap from which they can't escape: They have developed expensive drug habits that require the vast amounts of cash, or they have spent so long away from the workforce that the hole in their résumé makes reentry into the bourgeois workforce extremely difficult.

Chapter Eight

Sexually Transmitted Diseases

For the most part if you engage religiously in safe-sex practices, you will not contract a sexually transmitted disease. However, the only completely risk-free sexual encounter would involve two men standing on opposite sides of the bed, watching each other and gratifying themselves. There is no such thing as zero-risk sex.

Even if you are 100% committed to safe sex, shit happens. Rubbers break, unprotected oral sex can lead to exposure to HIV via small cuts in the mouth, saliva does not carry HIV but does carry hepatitis, and lots of nasty little creatures love to jump from body to body. If you are sexually active, it is best to get comprehensively tested for all STDs, including HIV, every six months. This can be done either at a doctor's office or, if you wish to keep the information out of the hands of present or potential insurers, at a metropolitan clinic.

STDs are not inevitable, but the more sex and the more sex partners you have, the higher your odds of catching one. The most important thing to know is how to protect yourself from STDs (see the safe-sex basics in chapter 3), but there are no guarantees. As such, you need to know a little about these diseases in case you come down with one. Listed below are common STDs, their symptoms, and information on treatment.

Gonorrhea

Gonorrhea is one of the most prevalent sexual diseases in America. The number of cases has spiked upward in recent years. It is a localized infection usually found in the penis, rectum, or throat. Occasionally it is found in the eye, the most dangerous place for the infection to take root. Gonorrhea does not *always* display symptoms, especially in the throat, but usually it is impossible to miss. In the penis, gonorrhea can cause a puslike discharge and severe pain during urination or orgasm. (It is possible to have severe pain while urinating and not have gonorrhea; the most likely cause would be a urinary tract infection. Either way, if it hurts, you need to see the doctor.) In the anus the puslike discharge can also be present, as well as rectal soreness long after your last sexual encounter. Oral gonorrhea is difficult to detect, as sometimes there are no symptoms. Gay men are most at risk for oral gonorrhea, as oral sex is usually performed without condoms.

If you do not treat gonorrhea and the symptoms go away, it does not mean you are cured. Gonorrhea is not like a cold, it does not go away. If you have it, you are infectious until you are treated. And even if you don't care about the health of others, you should still get treated; having gonorrhea, even without symptoms, is a constant tax on your immune system.

Gonorrhea is treated with certain kinds of penicillin. Shots in the ass used to be the usual treatment, but now the disease is cured with a single "magic bullet" pill. Do not attempt to self-medicate from leftovers in your bathroom cabinet. The medicine you receive from your doctor or the clinic is specifically designed to kill gonorrhea. In addition to taking the pill, individuals need to abstain from sex for ten days after treatment to ensure they do not infect someone else.

Syphilis

Syphilis is far rarer than gonorrhea but much more dangerous. There are usually no symptoms that can be linked directly to the bug; most likely, infection will result in a period of lethargy, achiness, slight fevers, and perhaps a noticeable skin eruption or hair loss—any and all of which could be attributed to a variety of causes. If undiagnosed and untreated, syphilis works behind the scenes of the immune system, potentially attacking any part of the body but most often causing blindness or heart or nervous system problems. Only testing can tell you if you have been exposed.

The treatment for syphilis, as with gonorrhea, is a form of penicillin in pill form. Again, you should not try to cure yourself; instead, take the prescribed medications exactly as directed.

Hepatitis

Each year, hepatitis becomes more of a threat as newer and more toxic strains spread around the world. The virus attacks the liver, and symptoms arise as some form of liver problem—a yellow cast to the whites of the eyes and the skin, dark brown urine, pale feces. Hepatitis also causes fatigue, nausea, and lack of appetite.

Hepatitis A is the most common strain. It can be transmitted through food or water tainted with feces—if you ever wondered, this is why the sign in the restaurant bathroom says EMPLOYEES MUST WASH HANDS. Hepatitis B is the most common strain among gay men and is far more powerful than A (though with the same basic symptoms). Other strains, now identified as C through G, are rarer but probably not for long.

The best cure for hepatitis is rest and "clean living." The liver needs time to repair the damage and clean out the toxins, and this is difficult if you don't help it out. It's important to eat well and avoid excess fats, take a vitamins such as Source Naturals' Life Force, with many liver-supporting nutrients, that will aid in the recovery process, get plenty of rest, and, most importantly, avoid drugs and alcohol. In most cases recovery is complete. But with Hepatitis B you can be a carrier for life, meaning anyone engaging in sex with you is at risk of infection. Hepatitis C, the most dangerous, can often be cured with injections of a drug called interferon.

The doctor or clinic can diagnose hepatitis and tell you which strain it is. Hepatitis vaccines are now available for some strains, and if you test negative for this disease, you are strongly advised to get the vaccines.

Chlamydia

Chlamydia, the most common sexual disease in America, often displays the same symptoms as gonorrhea—a puslike discharge and pain during urination or orgasm. Other times, though, it displays no symptoms at all. When you are tested for STDs you will be tested for chlamydia and, if necessary, treated with antibiotics.

Intestinal Parasites

Intestinal parasites are most often found in men who engage in oral-anal contact, manifesting as diarrhea or gas, or with no symptoms at all. Intestinal parasites are most dangerous to people with already compromised immune systems, as they can impair the body's ability to absorb nutrients, spread to vital organs, and generally wreak havoc.

If you have an intestinal parasite, the STD clinic cannot handle your problem. You'll need to visit your doctor.

Herpes

Before HIV, herpes was the scourge of sexually active people, both gay and straight. Practically everybody has some form of herpes virus in his body, manifesting, depending on the type of herpes, as something as mild as a cold sore on the lip to something as extreme as a painful, oozing sore on the genitals. Acyclovir, the most effective medicine in controlling outbreaks of herpes, is available over the counter, but if you think you might have herpes, you should still consult a doctor, who can tell you if you have herpes simplex, the basic cold sore herpes, or the more dangerous genital herpes. (Acyclovir controls the symptoms, but there is no cure for herpes.)

Herpes is spread through physical contact, usually with the sores or their discharge. The disease is often quiescent, meaning there are no visible sores. Quiescent herpes is harder to transmit, though not impossible. Hard living or psychological stress can cause quiescent herpes to become an outbreak of sores.

Venereal Warts

Venereal warts, like all warts, are a viral infection. Unprotected anal sex is just about the only way to get them. On the penis they occur as clusters of small bumps around the base; in the anus they are bumps or, left untreated, clusters of lumps on the walls of the rectum. Venereal warts must be burned off or burned out of your rectum, often with electricity. There is no medicine to take for them, and applying over-the-counter wart medicine to your penis will do nothing. As with herpes there is no cure for venereal warts. Once removed, the warts may or may not come back, so the painful procedure to remove them may have to be repeated.

Crabs

Crab lice present no major long-term health threat, but anyone who has ever had them will tell you that dealing with them is more difficult than dealing with most STDs. Crabs are not a disease, but they are usually spread through sexual contact. They live on and around body hair, especially pubic hair, and are so small they are virtually invisible to the eye. If you have crab lice, you'll know it. They live on dead skin, which they constantly scrape off you, causing an itching sensation so extreme as to be painful.

Crabs are the one STD you can diagnose yourself. If you find yourself with a severe itch in your pubic region, clip a few of your pubic hairs and examine them by stretching them out straight one by one. If you see a slight whitish bump or bumps on the hair, try to brush it off lightly. If it does not come off, changes are it is an egg from the louse.

If you catch crabs, the first thing to do is to get an over-the-counter treatment like A-200. This is a parasiticide expressly designed to kill lice and their eggs. Then take *all* clothes you have worn, *all* bedding you have slept on, and *all* linens you have used to the Laundromat. Don't drop them off to be washed by the laundry, as the sterilizing that is necessary won't be done. Wash everything as you normally would and then dry everything on the hottest setting for an hour. If you have worn items that need to be dry-cleaned, toss them unlaundered in the hot dryer for an hour and then have them dry-cleaned. Wash bath mats, towels, dishcloths, everything. Clean the house thoroughly using disinfectants and bleach.

Once you have clean clothes, apply the medication to your body as instructed. Remember, although lice congregate in pubic hair, they can be all over your body, so apply the medication anywhere you have hair. It is a good idea to shave off facial hair and even body hair. You need to be thorough, because if as many as two lice survive to procreate, all your efforts will have been in vain, and you will have to repeat the whole gruesome process.

Getting Medical Care

If you want to get tested for STDs, you have two options: visit your primary doctor or visit an STD clinic. There are many reasons you might not want to see your primary physician about an STD. You may be worried he will think poorly of you or give you a lecture, or you may be afraid the information will be harvested by the Medical Information Bureau and disseminated to potential health insurers. Moreover, getting in to see the doctor can take days or longer, whereas STD clinics operate on a walk-in basis.

If you live in a smaller community, you may be hesitant to be seen at or near the STD clinic (sometimes still called the VD clinic). If so, you might want to drive to the nearest big city. You can usually find the number for the clinic nearest you in the phone book. Look first in the city or county government listings under Department of Health.

When you call the clinic you will probably get a recording instead of a person. The recording will tell you the clinic's location and hours of operation. You are best off going first thing in the morning and waiting outside until the clinic opens. Monday mornings are usually the busiest time at the clinic.

You may be afraid to go to the clinic for fear that workers will treat you like a pariah, or that you will see or be seen by people you know, or that you will be surrounded by "lower orders" who go to the STD clinic not for secrecy but because they cannot afford a doctor. Fear not: The STD clinic is one of the few egalitarian institutions remaining in America. You will not be the only "nice boy" present.

When you go to the clinic take a magazine or book with you; you may not be able to concentrate on what you are reading, but at least you will have something to keep you occupied if you have to wait a lengthy time, which is often the case. People are sometimes called out of the order in which they arrived. If this happens, you are not being "cut in on." These are usually people returning for test results who don't need the intake process.

When you check in you will be issued a number and called up by that number instead of your name. When you are called you will usually see a nurse practitioner or physician's assistant, rather than a doctor. That person will ask you what he needs to know. Answer fully and honestly, otherwise there is no point in your being there. Remember, the staff members are not there to judge you but to help you. The fact is, they like you better when you tell them everything than when you hold back, because without the proper information they can't do their job effectively.

Swabs will be taken from your rectum, penis, and throat. Blood will be taken for the syphilis test. They will ask if you know your HIV status. If you do not, they will ask if you would like to be tested. Some clinics also offer free Hepatitis B vaccines. You will be asked about your sex partners; if you know their names and phone numbers and don't wish to contact them yourself, the clinic can do so without identifying you as the person from whom they may have contracted (or to whom they may have given) an STD. Should you wish to contact your partners yourself, just say so. You do not need to notify your partners that you went to the clinic and are waiting for results, but if any of your tests come back positive, you have a moral obligation to let them know.

The clinic will ask for a phone number at which they can contact you. As a general rule, the clinic will only call if something comes up positive. The exception is with HIV; you usually must receive the results of that test in person. You will often be given a phone number to call after a given period of time, usually a week, if you cannot stand the suspense. This results line will give you your test results for non-HIV STDs over the phone.

Before you leave the clinic you will probably be given two medications. The first is the one-shot magic bullet pill discussed earlier. This pill cures gonorrhea and chlamydia, and you are usually asked to take it on the spot. The other medication is a weeks' worth of pills for syphilis. Some people elect not to take the second medicine until they get their results. Unless you have severe objections to antibiotics, though, it is best to start taking the pills immediately so that by the time you get the results you will be cured of whatever you had. You will also be told to abstain from sex for ten days after your visit to avoid infecting someone else.

The clinic is a depressing place; there is no arguing with that. The irony is that for all the safe-sex information in the world, sometimes there is no better deterrent to unsafe sex than a trip to the STD clinic.

HIV

Getting any of the social diseases discussed above can be uncomfortable, painful, embarrassing, inconvenient, and irritating. But all those diseases can be effectively treated. HIV, however, is not in the same ballpark. An HIV diagnosis is not the automatic death sentence it was a few years ago, but there is still no cure.

Getting tested
Deciding to take an HIV test is difficult. Even if you have been 100% safe, you can be anxious about your HIV status. If you have

had unsafe sex or even sexual contact with someone that might have accidentally led to HIV infection, you can be even more anxious.

The number 1 reason people use to not take the HIV test is denial. Many men who tell you that they are negative (a negative test means they do not have HIV) and believe it themselves do so only because they have never been tested and therefore never been told otherwise. Thus they are "officially" HIV-negative. Not knowing your status does not mean you are negative.

The number 2 reason is fear. *What if I am positive? My whole world will change, and my life is too messy right now to deal with that. I'll get tested when things calm down and I can handle the strain.* The fact is, nobody ever has his affairs in order well enough to easily handle news like an HIV-positive diagnosis. There is never a good time to get tested.

A regular HIV test is a necessity for every sexually active person, especially if that person is involved in a relationship that includes unsafe sex. You and your partner may have gone to the clinic together and both tested negative, then sworn to never sleep with anyone else so the two of you could have sex without rubbers. This is nice in theory, but countless men have made this deal and become infected because their partner did not hold up his end of the bargain. And many other men have gone years without knowing they were positive, only finding out when they discovered their lover's HIV medications hidden in the back of the linen closet. *If you are having sex, you need an HIV test at least once a year.* Consider it an insurance policy.

A home HIV test is better than no test at all, but if you test positive, the only counseling you get will be from the test-kit company, which will give you a list of resources over the phone along with your diagnosis. If you *must* avoid taking the test in a doctor's office or clinic, at the very least you should notify your closest friend and have him with you when you call for your results. If you test positive, you won't want to be alone. And even a negative result can be strangely traumatic.

Getting test results

At first, testing HIV-negative is like living through a major earthquake—there is a giddy sense that you have been "spared." But even this happy result has its downside, especially if you are young and engaged in unsafe behavior before your test. If that is the case, there is a danger that you will think you are immune and consequently able to practice unsafe behavior. As someone who tested negative several times before testing positive, I assure you this is not true. Another potential problem is that people who test negative sometimes suffer from survivor's guilt, similar to that experienced by Holocaust survivors.

Testing HIV-positive is, obviously, far worse than testing negative. If you do test positive, the result is going to put you into a state of shock for six months. This is how long it takes the human brain to absorb the blow of a major psychological trauma. Don't do anything rash—quit your job, sell all of your worldly possessions, run up $50,000 in credit card bills. Wait at least six months after your diagnosis before making major life decisions.

As stated earlier, a positive result is not the death sentence it was a few years ago. To be told you had HIV even as late as the mid 1990s was to be told there was, with absolute certainty, an early and gruesome death awaiting. The only variable was when. Today, however, there are medications that can not only prolong your life but also provide a quality of life equivalent to that of an HIV-negative person. Even so, there is no guarantee of long-term survival. In some people the virus mutates around the new drugs and the person dies of AIDS anyway. And some people never respond to the drugs at all, or get such horrible side effects that for them drugs might as well not exist.

Regardless of the effectiveness of medications, if you are positive, HIV will rule your life. This is not a scare tactic, this is fact. It will influence who has a relationship with you, the character of that relationship, and the sex you have. It will influence where you work—one of your primary considerations will be whether the company offers the type of insurance you need to get your medication. It will influence the risks you take, how your family and friends treat you, and on and on and on. Do not let anyone convince you that just because there are now effective treatments that HIV is no big deal. Anyone who tells you that is lying.

Coming out as HIV-positive

Finding out you are HIV-positive—hopefully an experience you will never have—entails another coming-out process, with the same steps and ego-strength building. You first have to acknowledge it to yourself. Then you have to tell your friends (and also your lovers). Then family, and then, perhaps, the world. Whereas it is important to be out in the world about being gay, sometimes it is best not to be out about being HIV-positive, as discrimination against you on this count can lead to a life-threatening loss of job and insurance—or worse.

Counseling and sometimes even therapy is invaluable after a positive diagnosis, though it is not always available in smaller communities, and even in larger ones there is often a waiting list. If you can't get counseling at the clinic or from your doctor, find a way to get it somewhere else.

The Most Important Thing

When you test positive for any STD, you have a moral obligation to notify any and every partner you can that you have been diagnosed with the STD and that he should get tested immediately. This is hardest to do when you are in a monogamous relationship and must tell your partner that not only have you been unfaithful, but you also may have given him an STD. Keeping it a secret so as not to risk losing him is a selfish act. If you do this, you are putting him in grave danger, possibly ruining his life. If you really love him, you won't let him go on thinking he is in perfect health when you know he is not. You'll tell him. (And if you don't really love him, you should tell him and then move on.)

part two

Being Out

Coming out is a process of exploration, learning new things and learning how to adapt to your new world. Learning and adapting is, obviously, a lifelong process, but at a certain point you will see in your mind a map of your new community and on that map, pointing right to the center, will be an arrow that reads YOU ARE HERE. Congratulations: You've established your new life.

As you settle in and the initial excitement dampens, there are some less dramatic and more practical things you need to know. Whereas the opening section of this book was about coming out, this section is about being out. This section will provide you with the information you need to integrate gayness into your fuller life, a life in which being gay does not have to be the be-all and end-all of your existence.

Love affairs for gay men are different from those of straight people—our cultural obsessions are different, and our encounters with authority are laced with an inherent danger. The higher presence of AIDS among gay men than among straight people (at least for now) requires us to build friendships and support systems that demand more of us than traditional friendships.

Chapter Nine

Your First Relationship

Chances are that you will not be out for long before the opportunity to have a relationship presents itself. This may come in any number of forms: An older man may offer you the keys to his heart, his house, and his car; you may go home with a man one night and find him up the next morning cooking breakfast, cleaning your house, and asking what time you'd like dinner. Or you may find yourself having the kind of sex that is so incredible that you can't help but mistake it for love. (None of these is likely to develop into a stable long-term relationship.)

Some people argue that gay men should settle down and behave themselves as soon as possible so that they can all move to the suburbs and buy minivans just like straight people. Others, including me, disagree. Your 20s (or, if you are older, your first few years as an out gay man) are for experimenting, exploring, and learning, not for settling down.

It is easy to fall in love when you have just come out. You are intoxicated by the abundance of new experiences and loving your new life. The addition of a man to the mix seems only natural. Some people get lucky; they meet someone early in the coming-out process with whom they have internal harmony—sexually, mentally, and emotionally—and grow together rather than apart over these transforming exploratory years. In reality, though, in the early stages of coming out, you are far more likely to meet a lifelong friend than a long-term lover. First relationships almost never work out. Usually, the best you can hope for is a period of good sex that turns into friendship.

If you are in a new city filled with people you don't know, or if you already lived in the city but don't know many (or any) gay people, it is usually easier to meet people for sex than friendship. Single men, gay or straight, naturally get lonely. And the easiest way to assuage that loneliness is with a pickup—someone to talk to, someone to touch, someone you can be with *right now*. Sometimes we are so grateful to a man for easing our loneliness that we grab onto him like a life preserver. Remember, though, that raw need is almost always visible, and nothing in the world will repel a man faster than you clutching onto him like said life preserver. Any man who is the recipient of that kind of neediness will know instinctively that you are not looking for him, you are just looking for someone, anyone. Eventually, and more likely sooner than later, he will run from you. In the process you may lose not just the lover he never could have been but the friend he might have been.

Many gay men find that the bulk of their friends were people they met and had sex with and then later became friends with. Usually the sex was only marginal, but the conversation afterward was good, leading the men to discover that although they didn't click sexually, they had other things in common that made it worthwhile to keep in contact. When you can do this you have reached a maturity level that few straight people ever get to. If you approach your first relationship as a potential friendship rather than a potential long-term relationship, you'll be better off all the way around.

The biggest mistake people make with their first love is to rush it. You may feel that you are certain of your feelings and that you know the other person as well as you need to in order to make the jump. After all, you've spent every waking minute together for a whole week now! This is especially common among younger men, whose sense of time is telescoped and for whom a week with someone is an eternity of mutual exploration and discovery. Rarely do relationships succeed when the partners move in together after a brief fling, so even if you meet someone and fall for him and feel sure he is "the one," take it slow. If he is the one, he'll still be there in 12 months. And if he is, *then* you can talk about the next step beyond dating.

The fact is, you often learn more about yourself from the relationships that fail than from those that succeed. When you look back on a disastrous experience after the pain has receded, you can see a pattern of behavior in both yourself and your partner. If you are smart, you will learn from your behavior and avoid repeating it in the future. Some people are easily drawn into "fight-and-fuck" relationships, others into codependency, and still others are soft touches for a sob story and continually find themselves taken advantage of. The point is, your first relationship is likely to end, possibly badly. If you learn from your mistakes, you have a chance to find lasting love.

In a later and broader chapter on relationships, I'll discuss negotiating the terms of a working relationship. Right now, though, it's just important for you to know that the early stages of coming out are a critical time for you. You need to not only watch others but to also watch yourself and find out what you are really looking for.

Chapter Ten

Gay Subcultures

In small cities there is usually only one gay place. Everyone goes there and for the most part gets along, if only because they have no alternative. There is no segregation by lifestyle, looks, or age.

In big cities, however, there is often a gay ghetto, a section of town populated by gay and gay-friendly people. (Usually it is a marginal area taken over by gay men who work hard to raise the quality of life, nearly always succeeding.) A gay ghetto provides strength in numbers, allowing gay men the luxury of splitting into subcultures, much the same way a black ghetto accommodates both "superfly guys" and "Philadelphia Negroes," or a Jewish ghetto accommodates both Orthodox and Reform Jews. The gay ghetto allows gay people to pursue a life that excludes straight people—and sometimes also large portions of the gay population as well.

Below is a "tour" of the most prevalent gay subcultures. The most important thing to remember is tolerance. You may be horrified or doubled up on the floor laughing after encountering one of these groups, but "live and let live" is the cornerstone of a free society. Always keep in mind Voltaire's maxim, loosely translated, "I do not like what you do, but I will defend to the death your right to do it."

The World of Drag

Gay men have been dressing up as women at least since ancient Greece. In New York in the 1920s, drag balls were major social events for the gay underground, and for a wide swath of straight society too. In the 1960s drag queens picked up rocks and bottles and attacked police during a raid on the Stonewall Inn, a New York City gay bar, igniting the Stonewall riots and sparking the modern gay rights movement. In the 1990s young gay men turned drag on its head, stripping away its Judy Garland and Barbra Streisand lip-synching warhorse persona and remaking it with characters of their own creation, mad divas who not only acted out the self-destructive qualities drag had celebrated for decades but who also parodied that behavior, making a comedy out of pining away for unrequited love in an age in which people were dying because of sex.

Through the ages, gay men have explored their feminine sides through drag, sometimes because they really wanted to do so, other times because the dominant culture brainwashed them into thinking they were more woman than man.

Drag's finest hour came in the headiest days of gay liberation. At Stonewall and after, drag queens played the role of buxom Britannia, first over the battlements, rainbow flag in hand, leading the troops to victory. But as time went by and gay culture became more assimilated into mainstream culture, as the American middle class began to accept homosexuality as long as it wasn't "thrown in their faces," the sympathies of many gay men turned from celebrating drag to actively discouraging it as "sending the wrong message."

Some gay men believe the classic drag queen of the big-hair-and-sequins variety has been left behind by history, that playing such an overly exaggerated feminine role is no longer necessary. Whatever you believe, keep in mind that the more tolerant social climate you are coming out in is the direct result of sacrifices made by these drag queens.

For many gay men drag is a once-in-a-lifetime thing, something done to get their "gay card." This once-in-a-lifetime event almost invariably takes place on Halloween, the gay Saturnalia when any-thing and everything can and should be turned on its head. Some men go all the way, shaving their beard, chest, legs, and anything else necessary to produce a shocking verisimilitude of womanhood. Other men prefer to simply engage in a light bout of genderfuck, in which a clearly masculine man puts on a dress to make a statement that he is not afraid that he will lose that masculinity if he puts on a dress (an idea grunge-rocker Kurt Cobain carried to the straight world after his friendly and positive experiences with gay people.)

Much of the prejudice today against old-school drag queens is eco-nomic. Old-school drag is a downscale world. Hangouts are usually dank, seedy bars filled with aging alcoholics who relish reenactments of the lives of tragic female stars. Annual contests for emperor and empress invade the rest of the gay community via rented limos or bor-rowed Cadillacs, advertising a sense of taste and class that others scoff at as hopelessly outdated and tacky.

Nonetheless, much of what the drag court does in its contests is community-oriented; money made at various shows and court events is often poured into the coffers of AIDS-service organizations. Consequently, drag queens can find themselves feeling, in the broad-er gay community, a bit like Belle Watling in *Gone With the Wind*—your money's good but you yourself aren't welcome.

The "new" drag often takes place in clubs catering to a younger crowd and is more interested in creating new personas than re-creat-ing old stars. New drag is still about exploring one's feminine side, but it's also about mining the self-destructive cultural baggage that comes with tightly defined gender roles.

The one thing drag queens won't stand for is open contempt. You may find the whole thing pathetic, but a drag queen has found a meas-ure of dignity in what she is doing. (Drag queens prefer to be referred to as she or her.) You may not have what it takes to smile indulgently while some bewigged and sequined beast lip-synchs *I Will Survive*, but a sneer or snicker will get you clocked with a heel. If you display con-tempt with drag in a drag setting, don't be surprised if you can't get a drink, get overcharged, or suffer the wrath of a performer (first-rate drag performers are notorious for their rapierlike wit). If you are particularly obnoxious, you'll probably be asked to leave.

The Leather World

In the 1950s an artist working under the name Tom of Finland began creating a gay fantasy world full of young pumped-up mustache-sporting men in black leather jackets, Nazi-esque caps, and tight jeans—the Marlon Brando biker movie *The Wild Ones* made queer. After the onset of gay liberation, gay men searched for a recognizable identity not based on the *Boys in the Band* look of fluttery scarves and overprocessed hair. Tom of Finland's drawings became the archetype for a whole new way of looking, acting, and being gay.

Leather and S/M are often lumped together as one thing, but they are not necessarily so. Leather is mostly about what you wear. S/M is a way of life. Before AIDS there were numerous bars devoted solely to the practice of hard-core S/M. These bars usually featured dark back rooms equipped with slings, cuffs, and harnesses, and bathrooms with outsized troughs (for men to lie in and be peed on), and sometimes slings in the front room, dramatically lit and occupied by someone willing to let anyone do anything to him in view of all as part of his kick. S/M is now something practiced, for the most part, privately, whether in individuals' bedrooms or playrooms (rooms in peoples' houses rigged for use exclusively as an S/M dungeon), or at private sex clubs devoted to S/M. S/M practitioners meet in leather bars now, but you need not fear that going to a leather bar will result in abduction, rape, and fisting (as it might in a typical Tom of Finland drawing).

If you wish to go to a leather bar, be aware that some are more restrictive about dress code than others. You can go to the Eagle in San Francisco wearing white tennis shoes with jeans and a leather jacket, whereas the Loading Dock, in the same neighborhood, wouldn't let you in. If you go to a leather bar on a weekend night, you will find some men in full leather, some in police or military uniforms (which may or may not be real), and some in a leather jacket, jeans, a plain T-shirt, and boots. As with all of the gay subcultures, be polite, even if it's not for you. No snickering is allowed.

Leather and uniform bars are among the few places in which you may need to know about the hankie code, described in the appendix of this book. The code is the means by which men with specialized tastes let each other know exactly what they are looking for so that no time is wasted making small talk with the wrong person. Anything worn on the left means top (insertive partner), and anything worn on the right means bottom (receptive partner). Some men may not flag their exact preferences, either because they are discreet or because they are eclectic in their tastes, but will instead indicate top or bottom with a cock ring, chain, or some other visible device looped through the epaulet of their leather jacket. Or they may use keys hooked to a belt loop and tucked in either the right or left pants pocket.

As a general rule, men into the leather scene are older than those on the dance and club circuits. You might think this is because they're too old for the dance scene, but for the most part these men have either tired of younger men, grown jaded with "vanilla" sex, or have always preferred the company of older men. (Most of the young men involved in the leather scene are not interested in partners their own age, preferring men over the age of 30, 40, or even 50.)

S/M sex can be as vanilla as role-playing accompanied by light bondage and spanking or as extreme as blood sports, where the bottom is immobilized and "tortured" to the point where blood is drawn. S/M *appears* to be about domination, pain, and cruelty, but in fact it is about limits and trust, and the expansion of both within a relationship, be that relationship a few hours or several years in duration. For the men in this community, the key phrase is *safe, sane, and consensual.* In other words, I may beat you with a paddle but only if I know you want to be beaten. It is about raping the willing, not the unwilling. S/M sex always has a safe word so that the submissive partner can scream "No" and "Stop" without actually meaning it. The safe word serves as code for "it's time to stop" and is usually something odd and innocuous, like *watermelon* or *Rolodex.*

If you find yourself drawn to S/M sex, tread lightly as you begin your explorations. More than in any other world, you need to proceed cautiously, as there are hangers-on who are sadists of the sociopathic variety who do not respect the boundaries of S/M, let alone the laws of society. Bartenders and regulars at the tougher leather bars are good people to chat up, as is anybody with a title, usually in the form of a vest or belt studded with contest wins like Mr. Chicago Leather 1998 or Leather Daddy's Boy 1999. These are men who are into the scene, well-known, and usually willing to advise anyone looking to learn more about the S/M world. They can also tell you who in the scene you should avoid at all costs.

Bears

In contemporary gay culture there are few unpardonable sins. Eighty-year-old men being "escorted" by their 18-year-old "companions," partying on a nonstop basis, and getting down on your knees in certain toilets in certain bars and waiting for a certain brand of gratification have all been accepted by sophisticated gay men without the bat of an eyelash. Yet watch an obese man cross paths with these same sophisticates and you won't need to wait long for the shock, horror, and disgust to manifest. In gay society, even more than in straight society, the one great sin is obesity.

Furthermore, for a long time being gay meant purging yourself of your roots—roots that symbolized everything savage and backward and cruel and ignorant that you were running away from. As a gay man you had one choice: You moved to the city and you turned yourself into a refined, polished, cosmopolitan man because it made you the polar opposite of all the people who made your life hell. You dropped everything you ever knew, even the good stuff, and became a bitchy queen.

The Bear culture is a reply to this, a way for men who don't fit the gay ideal to create a world in which they are the norm and not the sore thumb. Bears merge the never-changing blue-collar and rural look of John Deere hats, flannel shirts, and other warm, practical clothing, with basic leather attire like jackets and key rings. Bear culture is an acknowledgment that the predominant gay culture has become corrupt, shallow, and cruel and that certain values and pleasures have been left behind—the blue-collar work ethic, the notion of sticking together as community and helping those in need, and the enjoyment of rural pastimes like fishing, hunting, and camping.

Bear bars are often the most comfortable places to be for a gay man. The spaces Bears create are welcoming (to everyone other than the snickering queen). A Bear bar is not only a place to find Bears but also gay men with strong rural roots and identities whose "butch" clothing and 4-by-4 trucks are not fashion accessories but a way of life.

Walking into a Bear bar in no way means that you are self-identifying as a "chubby chaser," as many gay men seem to think. The spirit of the Bear bar is friendliness, and most passes that will be made at you are just that—friendly. The ultimate compliment in a Bear bar is to hear "Woof" as you walk by. All that is required of you in return is friendliness, even when rejecting an advance. As in any situation, if someone is too aggressive, don't hesitate to be curt in response; there are Bears and there are Buffaloes, and nobody likes a Buffalo. If you are being mashed in a Bear bar, all it takes is a quick look around with an evident plea for help on your face and your attacker will not trouble you for long.

Being a Sissy

Many gay men go through a feminine phase. (This is becoming less frequent as the messages of gay liberation reach young people at earlier ages.) All the same, many gays without alternative role models absorb the cultural message—delivered by everyone from schoolyard bullies to cinematic stereotypes—that gays are sissies. It is difficult not to be influenced by this message and act accordingly, swishing and camping it up. For some men this is just a phase, part of trying on personas and discarding them as they find their true identities. For others sissiness is a natural state.

One of the ironies of gay liberation is that it has made the genuine sissy even more isolated, as other gay men now look at sissies the way they sometimes look at drag queens, thinking, *Why is he doing this? We don't have to do that anymore.* Many gays react with loathing to the hysteria of Richard Simmons or Nathan Lane's portrayal of an old queen in *The Birdcage.* The feeling is that these men are capitalizing on straight America's desire to have gay men around but only as eunuchs and clowns.

Many sissies go into high-end retail sales, learning the nuances of "the finer things in life," adopting an arrogance born of aesthetic superiority. They are beloved by the same women (and occasionally men) who adore Simmons and Lane, they make good money, and they find a place in society where they may still be mocked but are not powerless. Some even take up bodybuilding, astonishing the world when the voice of Marilyn Monroe emanates from the mouth of Arnold Schwarzenegger.

It is important for gay men to remember that, for the most part, queeny or sissified behavior is learned, not natural. It is not necessary to be a sissy just because you're gay. But if you *are* a natural-born sissy, then be proud of it, but be prepared to receive significant attitude not only from straights but also from gays.

The Queer-Punk Scene

As one gay generation was presiding over the last days of disco, another was spending its adolescence with music a world away from the compositions of Sylvester and Donna Summer. Growing up with the music of punk rock and new wave, the next generation was not interested in cowbells and tambourines or hi-NRG or divas shrieking over the latest *thumpa-thumpa* dance-floor hit. This new queer punk generation found its voice and recognition in the days of ACT UP and Queer Nation political activism, and while those groups are not as prominent as they once were, the social and sexual underground they created lives on.

Like any generational rebellion, queer punk was a young people's reaction to the world they were expected to join, the bourgeois world of business and property ownership, a world they were either not interested in or, during George Bush's recession, unable to join. These young men spent the 1980s watching nothing happen but death and decided it was time to dance again, to have sex again, to take drugs (other than for AIDS treatment) again, to build a new, alternative subculture with its own music, its own fashions, and its own haunts. The queer-punk world today is far less political than during its early years, probably because two terms with a liberal president have made life for gay people far more pleasant than it used to be.

Like Bears, queer punks stole fashion ideas from their clone predecessors—leather jackets, jeans, and boots. But queer punks reached all the way back to the original "dirty biker" roots, trashing and defacing the clothing to create an aggressively downscale look that would terrify the Reaganauts who saw them in televised demonstrations. Piercings, formerly limited to zones where they could be concealed during one's day job at the bank, branched out and colonized noses, eyebrows, lips, and even tongues (if you're making a face right now, you've never gotten a blow job from someone with a pierced tongue). Music was selected on how well it went with one's drugs, be it acid house with LSD or techno anthems with X.

For people who grow up feeling "alternative" for reasons above and beyond their sexuality, the queer-punk world offers a place where individuality is more important than fashion's latest trend. Queer punk thrives in New York's East Village, San Francisco's South of Market, and in various anti–West Hollywood bastions in Los Angeles. Where there is insufficient grooviness for queer punks to support their own scene, they can often be found sharing turf with Bears.

The great irony is that this subculture, which only ten years ago was despised by its gay elders for its "slacker" ways and the time it wasted playing with computers, is now at the center of the digital boomtown, making more money—without abandoning a single nose ring—than any previous gay generation or current gay subculture.

The Circuit

Just as television shows run sweeps-week scandal pieces, usually about sex or prostitution, so too do gay publications run shocking exposés, invariably covering the circuit. Such articles are replete with juicy details about drug-soaked, sex-laden weekends at hotels in sunny destinations, where beautiful young men and wealthy not-so-young men from across the country congregate, ostensibly for a night of dancing to the music of a legendary DJ, but actually to take off their shirts and astound each other with their tan, plucked musculature, and, if the drugs allow them to so much as say hello to a stranger, find one or more hot sex partners.

The tone of the articles is invariably censorious; we are treated to walk-throughs of the lost weekend alongside a young stud who loses a boyfriend to someone hotter than himself, or we get to watch some buff Iowa farmboy fall into a K-hole. It is all sordid and accompanied by lots of pictures of hot men, which provide an odd counterpoint to the words that paint such a bleak and unappetizing picture.

These articles are popular for the same reason that books like Michelangelo Signorile's *Life Outside* or Gabriel Rotello's *Sexual Ecology* are popular— they give an intimate peek into a world most of us will never enter. The tragedy of these books and articles is that they are a throwback to the days of books like *Everything You Always Wanted to Know About Sex*, in which the only way for a gay man to find out anything useful was to swallow the facts with a large spoonful of censure and disgust from the writer.

The circuit is a floating world all its own, consisting of a set of public parties around the country. Some gay men attend only when the pleasure barge arrives near their home. Others, more prosperous or well-subsidized, follow the party as it moves around the country. In its own way the circuit is a community; many of the attendees see each other only at circuit events, occasionally forming friendships despite the general "hit-and-run" atmosphere of the scene.

There is a group of men whom Armistead Maupin irrevocably labeled in his writing as the "A-gays," men with looks, taste, a sense of adventure, and, most importantly, an endless supply of money to refine, improve, and subsidize the other three qualities. While not all A-gays are circuit queens, the core of the circuit, and indeed the core of what disapproving writers despise so much about it, is composed of A-gays. Part of this dislike is simple human jealousy. The A-gays have it all, and with men struggling to have any of it, this rarely breeds sympathy.

Circuit parties are, technically speaking, public events. Anybody is free to purchase a ticket and attend a circuit party, but to formally enter this competition and be accepted as in, you must be young, handsome, in superior physical condition, well-hung, and have either the funds for expensively priced event tickets and outrageously priced drinks, or the hustle to find someone who does. Furthermore, you will be required to follow fashion with a monomania that leaves you with little or no time for more intellectual pursuits, as you ensure that you have at all times the right hair, the right clothes, and, most importantly to the style queens on the circuit, the right shoes. Your exercise regimen, your diet, and even your intake of legal supplements and illegal drugs will revolve around maintaining not fitness and health but a perfectly buff body. In short, if you are not one of those who was born having it all, you will find yourself knocking yourself out to play catch-up with those who were.

There are decent people on the circuit, beautiful and successful men whose only flaw is their wish to be surrounded by no one other than gay men as perfect and removed as themselves. In the nicest men you meet on the circuit, the great sin is not arrogance but obliviousness: They take so completely for granted that they are "the bomb" that anybody who criticizes their lifestyle must only be crying sour grapes.

A Few Circuit Stories

Andy, a man I know, was slim and unpopular with the circuit boys he wanted to hang out with. He got on steroids, bulked up, became an escort, and suddenly had the looks and money to live the circuit life. He met someone at the White Party in Palm Springs who became his boyfriend. One night, high on drugs, the boyfriend suggested a walk along the cliffs at

Land's End in San Francisco. Racing up the hill behind his new boyfriend, exultantly whacked out on crystal meth and oblivious to danger, Andy slipped and fell 400 feet. He spent several months in the hospital, lost 40 pounds, and had substantial nerve damage on one side of his body that made it difficult for him to regain the muscle he'd had before the accident. The boyfriend dropped him, saying he "just couldn't take all this." Andy, it seems, was no longer the sort of boyfriend this man wanted. Andy's other circuit friends disappeared after one visit to the hospital.

SF Weekly did a cover piece in which a female reporter followed some San Francisco men to a circuit party. They were all young, professional, had their careers on track, and saw circuit parties as places to blow off steam by taking drugs, dancing all night, and having wild sex. One of these young men told the reporter that his life would be complete, if only sometime during the weekend one of the DJs would play the disco version of Olivia Newton-John's "Hopelessly Devoted to You." And do you *really* care what someone who worships Olivia Newton-John thinks about your shoes?

It is undeniably true that there are many negatives to the circuit. Let it be said, though, that like many gay men, if I were at a circuit party, I would not turn down an invitation to get laid by one or more of the chiseled young hunks in attendance. It is hard to find anybody on the circuit who is willing to condemn it and just as hard to find anybody not on the circuit to endorse it. If you are "in," the circuit is fun; you are officially approved, endorsed, and stamped as Grade AAA beef to be envied by all who are not. But if the circuit becomes your life, to the exclusion of all other interests, you are going to be miserable when a page of the calendar turns and you are suddenly "out."

Conclusion

Conservative gay writers like Bruce Bawer wish that certain of the gay subcultures, like leather men and drag queens, would just go away so that right-wingers couldn't film them at parades and use them to paint an admittedly skewed portrait of homosexuality that they use to bolster their fund-raising tactics. But it is not the fault of any of these subcultures that the far right plays dirty pool, and to suppress any of these groups is to hand the far right a victory.

We do all have to get along. We are all gay, and to our enemies we are all the same. Jesse Helms is not grading us on a curve, giving you five extra points because you don't wear a dress or a leather harness. It no longer appears that the day of the "big roundup" is coming, but there are many of us who lived through the days when that seemed, if not likely, then possible, or at least not unthinkable. It was not so many years ago that the idea of tattooing or even quarantining all HIV-positive people was given serious consideration, and many of those who proposed and considered it are still in positions of power.

Maybe the discussion of gay subcultures is best summed up with a quote from Pastor Martin Niemoller, arrested by the Nazis during World War II: "In Germany, they came for the communists, and I didn't speak up because I wasn't a communist. Then, they came for the Jews, and I didn't speak up because I wasn't a Jew. Then, they came for the trade unionists, and I didn't speak up because I wasn't a trade unionist. Then, they came for the Catholics, and I didn't speak up because I was a Protestant. Then, they came for me, and by that time there was no one left to speak up."

Chapter Eleven

Too Young, Too Old, Too Ethnic

The Underage Gay

There are two situations where it is hard to be gay and underage. One, when you still live at home; two, when you don't.

As a general rule, the age of consent is 18; sex between one person below that age and another person at or above that age is considered statutory rape. You may be eager to have your first sexual experience with an older man, and you may be dismayed to find that he rejects you upon learning your age. This is not a rejection of you personally; it is a practical decision on his part based on fear of jail and the label *child molester*. You may well be the most mature and sophisticated 16-year-old in America, but your parents probably won't care about that, and the courts certainly will not.

If you are underage, you are much better off not pursuing older men—not only because you could get them in trouble but because there is a predatory class of men, albeit a small one, who are always on the lookout for young chickens to pluck. You may meet them online, and they may lure you across country with promises of a place to live and a warm bed, but once you arrive you may find that you aren't what they're looking for or that they want a quickie and then are done with you, and there you are, stuck, hundreds or even thousands of miles from home.

How much of an active gay life you have in your pre-legal teens will vary widely depending on geography and the climate at home. If you live in or near a big city, there are gay youth groups where you can meet other gay teens in a social environment not unlike a regular boys' or girls' club. Some big cities even have high schools exclusively for gay students. Services for gay youth are the one of the biggest advances in gay liberation in the last 20 years. (If you look at the chapter on young gays in the previous version of this book, you will find that the only suggestions for places to meet other gay teens are doughnut shops and hamburger stands where runaway boys hung out to meet "generous" older men.) The easiest way to make contact with gay youth groups is by searching the internet or calling the local gay hotline. (Almost any medium-size or larger city will have a gay hotline. Look in the yellow pages under *gay* or *crisis*.)

If you are living at home, your access to gay youth programs will depend a good deal on your relationship with your parents. If you are out to your parents, you should take advantage of every service available to you as a gay teen in your community. If not, attending gay youth events might be more difficult. Still, it is in your best interest to meet as many gay people, especially those your own age, as possible. You will not only make friends, but you will also develop a support network filled with other individuals who are experiencing the same things you are.

Sometimes being gay is enough to get you thrown out of the house or enough to make life in the house so unbearable, physically and mentally, that you are better off running away than enduring the beatings and other punishments you receive when your parents discover your sexuality. Running away is a last resort. It is not something to do because life at home is "a hassle." There is not one single adolescent in the entire world whose home life is not a hassle. Leaving home is something to be considered *only* when you are in real danger if you stay.

Running away to the big city should not be thought of as your first choice but as the last option for a desperate young person. If life at home becomes unbearable, you should seek refuge with a friend's family or with a relative who is in a position to go to court to take custody of and protect you. Another viable option is to throw yourself on the mercy of a teacher or counselor at school who can get you into foster care. Today, in many areas, gay teenagers are placed with gay foster parents, providing at least a little breathing room and a safe place to make plans for the future. (This is not the case in all areas.)

Even today, despite the volume of stories about the hopelessness and dreariness of life on the streets, kids still run away to the big city in hope of something better. The fact is, you will not find it. You are too young to get a place to live; without an address and phone number you will have a hard time finding a job; and having arrived in the city presumably with little if any money, you will quickly need to start peddling your ass to survive. Many of the men who prey on homeless boys insist on having unsafe sex because they are in the position to pay extra for it and don't really give a shit about their partner; thus, you could easily become infected with HIV within days of your arrival. Most cities are cold at night, and when you do not have the money for a place to live, you quickly find that taking drugs numbs the cold as well as the emotional pain you are feeling over having been cast out of your home and consequently needing to fuck old trolls just to get enough money for food. This is the way it *always* goes. Don't think you're going to be the exception. There is absolutely no chance that you will be "discovered" and turned into a star because, as you might have forgotten, you're not even old enough to sign a contract.

Don't think that the street is a place where the kids take care of each other, either. Most of the kids on the street are not gay kids but straight kids who have left physically abusive homes. Moreover, many of them are from environments where they have watched their drug-addicted parents enact scripts involving swearing their honesty up and down to people they always intended to rip off. These kids have memorized the scripts, and many of them are as in love with their drug of choice as their parents were. They will have no compunction about scamming you.

If you do land in the city, there are service agencies to help you, often run by gay people who have been on the streets themselves. The sooner you call one of these agencies, the better off you will be. Some agencies will even provide you with an address and a voice-mail number so that you can get a job and will assist you in finding housing.

Coming Out Older

An amazingly large number of gay men have heterosexual lives in their pasts. Many of them married young and had kids, often to deceive themselves as well as everyone else into believing they were straight, or at least to put themselves in a situation where being gay was no longer "possible." But you cannot go against nature, and sooner or later, if you are gay, that is the life you must lead.

As a consequence, many men find themselves entering the gay world after their formative years—often in their 30s, 40s, or 50s, and occasionally even later. There are several unique challenges that an older man faces upon coming out.

What you have missed can be both a blessing and a curse. In having missed out on the years where you were the hot boy, the center of other men's attention, you have missed out on an experience that can be tons of fun. On the other hand, having already reached the age where you are no longer automatically lusted after, without having spent formative years being lusted after, you do not have the experience of having lost something that men who came out earlier often go through. This can give you a maturity that other older gay men do not always achieve, as many of them are still seeking the same kind of approval from other men that was so easily gained in their 20s.

You have also not spent the years that your age peers have spent learning the inside arcana of gay life. You might not know the words to the songs in *A Chorus Line* or even who Stephen Sondheim is; you might not know which movie stars are gay or rumored to be gay; you might not get the joke when someone talks about a retro party where everybody wore painter's pants, web belts, and polo shirts. In some circles this will get you laughed at, but in others it is admirable—for gay men whose lives do not revolve around their sexuality, it can be a relief to find a man who hasn't devoted his life to making sure he is always wearing the right shoes.

Having lived a straight life as an adult, you have lived in a culture in which, to a great extent, being a man is enough. It may not have been incumbent to have kept your body in shape or to have a hairstyle, wardrobe, and glasses that were up-to-date. After you come out, however, these things will become important. There is, to be blunt, no upside to looking like someone who hasn't been to a clothing store since 1981. It will not be necessary for you to spend your life savings on new outfits, but you will want to get some basic, masculine clothes: a short leather jacket, clean and well-fitting jeans, white and black T-shirts, and some construction boots are a good start. These are the enduring basics of gay style and will serve you well in most casual situations. The older you are, the better off you are sticking with the basics. If you have missed having your wild gay 20s, do not try to make up for it in your 50s by wearing a striped Adidas athletic shirt and baggy raver pants or whatever "the kids are wearing" now. It will not work, and you will earn the scorn of both those younger than you and those your own age.

You may want a new haircut. It is not necessary to get a high-maintenance cut. Something short and masculine, perhaps even a near-crewcut, is best. If you wear glasses, let an eyewear professional help you find something that fits your face and is contemporary. (In general, if you have a round face, go with square glasses; if you have a square face, go with round glasses.)

Being in shape is important to gay men—arguably, we are obsessed with it. Some gay men select their friends on the basis of looks, though such creatures are so shallow that they are not worth impressing. All the same, you will find that women and men are different—women are far more likely to be attracted to what is inside a man and to accept the outside, whereas men tend to examine looks first and personality later. If you have let yourself go and you wish to now engage in an active sex and dating life, it is a good idea for you to start working out. (The gym is also a good place to meet men.)

Plastic surgery and makeup are often considered by gay men as they age, but the fact of the matter is that the evidence of both is usually blazingly obvious to all but the most naive. There is no concealing the fact that you are aging. Dying your gray hair blond or having your bags tucked will not make you look young; it will make you look old and frightening and obviously frightened of something you cannot avoid. No amount of money will change this—look at Sigfried and Roy. Some men prefer older men and some do not. The ones who do not will not be fooled by artifice; the ones who do are not looking for someone who is erasing the signs of character and age that they are seeking in their partners.

One of the biggest pitfalls awaiting the older man coming out is the temptation to try to make up for lost time. This can mean doing steroids and getting superpumped in order to attract young gymbots, or it can mean plunging into a relationship without letting it develop naturally. Nobody can make up for lost time; what is lost is lost. What you *can* do is find out just how much still awaits you and enjoy it to the fullest.

Another pitfall is that you have not developed the street smarts that other gay men have developed in their years in the community. Not every gay person is a saint; there are many men who will scam you, either quickly on a small scale or patiently and with diabolical cleverness on a large scale. You may be so relieved to be among the men you should have been among all along that in your rush to intimacy, you don't see that you are being taken advantage of. All gay men—not just older men—have to worry about this, which is why later in this book there is a chapter called Getting Scammed.

As with underage gays there are, in most big cities at least, social and support groups for older gay men. You may want to take advantage of these services. If nothing else, you will meet other individuals dealing with the same issues as yourself.

Gay and Ethnic

Gay minorities are quick to point out that they are doubly discriminated against in our society, first for their color and then for their sexuality. The sexual community that should accept them discriminates for the same reasons the dominant culture does, and the racial communities that should accept them are often more prejudiced against homosexuals than the white world.

On top of that, most gay ghettos, such as San Francisco's Castro, New York's Chelsea, and West Hollywood are predominantly white. Although the days are gone when bars would be so brazen as to discourage nonwhites from patronizing them by asking men of color for absurd amounts of identification, racism still exists, be it subtle or not so subtle. Every bar has its own feel, and an African-American, Latino, or Asian man will know quickly if he is not welcome—the bartender will be slow to serve him, other patrons will jostle him, if he puts his name on the blackboard for a game of pool, it will be "missed."

Racism exists. It is a fact. Wishing it away will not make it so. Segregation in the gay community does take place, especially in larger cities where there are enough gay people that a bar catering predominantly to Asians, African-Americans, or Latinos can do a booming business—not only with the members of that group but with white men who find them attractive.

Each generation inherits its predecessor's racism, and yet each generation is less racist than the last. When you encounter racist behavior in a bar or restaurant, let your friends know; word never spreads faster than in the gay community. Most gay people are politically progressive, and if word gets out that an institution is practicing or condoning racism, that business will usually either go under or be forced to change its ways in record time.

In most medium and large cities there are social and support groups for gay men of color. Sometimes the groups are quite specific, designed for Asians only or Latinos only or African-Americans only. You may want to take advantage of these services. If nothing else, you will meet other individuals dealing with the same issues as yourself.

Chapter Twelve

Cops, Fag Bashers, and Other Dangers

When you were growing up, you were told that policemen were your friends. If you were lost, you found a policeman. If a stranger approached you, you ran to a policeman. As you grew older, however, you probably realized that law officers do not always protect and serve as they are sworn to do. Anyone who has seen video of the Rodney King beating knows there are some who become policemen because it gives them an excuse to act like bullies, especially when dealing with ethnic or sexual minorities.

This may seem like an extreme statement, but I assure you it is not. For more than 12 years I lived in San Francisco, one of the most liberal U.S. cities, and every few years the police engaged in random outlaw violence. A few years ago a New Year's Eve party being run out of a warehouse without a permit by a group of gay men (as an AIDS benefit, no less) was violently broken up by cops who taped over their badge numbers and attacked the partygoers. Almost all the officers involved are still on the force. One can only surmise what it is like in the rest of the country.

The first edition of this book was written in a time far worse than our own. Back then police violence was not a shocking eruption every several years but a daily occurrence, especially in our community. That edition advised anybody going to a gay bar to be careful about hitting on someone who might be an undercover cop, cautioning that even though police rarely raided gay institutions anymore, it was advisable to be wary.

Even then, the authors noted, raids on gay bars were more likely to be election-time publicity stunts demonstrating that local authorities were "cracking down on sin" than an actual attack on the gay community.

Things have improved immeasurably since then; some police departments recruit new officers from the gay community and send gay cops to patrol gay neighborhoods as much as possible. This, however, is rare. As a gay man you should avoid contact with the police when possible because there is no guarantee that when you call the police you will be issued a gay or gay-friendly or even gay-neutral officer in response to your call for help.

At some point you are bound to come into contact with the police, either as an arrestee or as the victim of a crime. Read the remainder of this chapter carefully. No matter what course you choose in life, you are going to need this information.

Getting Busted

Public sex is still the number 1 reason gay men are arrested. Be aware that police occasionally run sting operations to crack down on public sex. Entrapment, technically defined as "when the conduct of law enforcement officers is such that it would induce a normally law-abiding person to commit an offense," is illegal. But before you engage in public sex, ask yourself this question: How many (presumably heterosexual) judges would rule that a "normally law-abiding person" would play with someone else's meat in a public toilet?

As a general rule, except for public sex, gay men are most likely to be arrested for the same reasons as anyone else: public drunkenness, drunken driving, drunk and disorderly conduct, domestic disputes, or drugs. All of these are run-of-the-mill occurrences in large- and medium-size cities and are not going to result in your immediate teleportation to prison. Remaining calm is the first order of business.

If you are arrested for any reason, remember that policemen considers themselves the long arm of the law. An affront to them is an affront to the system they have sworn to uphold, and vice versa. First and foremost, do not resist arrest. Doing so gives homophobic officers an excuse to subdue you with "necessary" force. Do not argue that there has been a mistake, and do not plead with them. Tell the truth about the basics—give your real name, as they will get it out of your wallet anyway. They will ask you if you have any drug paraphernalia in your pockets; this is for their own safety as, naturally, they don't wish to be stuck with a used needle when searching you. Remember that you have the right to remain silent. If they find drugs on you or in your car, say nothing. If you are arrested with someone else and one of you has possession of drugs, neither of you should say anything. It is a typical police procedure to separate the two of you at the station and interview you separately: "Your friend says the drugs are yours and that they're not for personal use but that you're going to sell them." Your only response should be, "I want to see my lawyer."

In other words, stay cool. Don't fight, don't argue, don't volunteer information aside from whether or not you have a needle on you. When asked if it's all right to search your vehicle or house, say, "No, I don't consent." They will try to convince you that the process will go easier if you cooperate—and it will, for them.

Getting out

If you have no record, you can be released on your own recognizance, meaning you are a generally law-abiding citizen and can be counted on to appear at your court date. If you are arrested on a Friday or Saturday night, you won't have this opportunity since the justice system, like any government bureaucracy, shuts down for the weekend. In this case you can usually get out on bail, which involves someone either posting bail for you, or, on a larger sum, paying a bail bondsman a fee and a deposit to bail you out. You are allowed at least one phone call; depending on circumstances, you might be placed in a holding tank and given additional time and phone calls to reach someone to bail you out. Long-distance calls are not an option nor, in many instances, for some unknown reason probably related to drug traffickers' fondness for them, can you dial prefixes that are assigned to cell phones. You may be wise to call a friend and ask him to make long distance and cellular calls for you.

If you can't get out and have to spend at least a night in jail, you may ask to be segregated from the general population because you're gay. If you are on medications that you cannot miss, let the officer in charge know whom he can call to have your medication delivered (if you cannot reach that person yourself). These requests are likely be honored because most municipalities have already spent enough money settling lawsuits filed by people who were mistreated in jail.

Getting a lawyer is a necessity; whether you hire one or accept a public defender will depend on your finances, the severity of the accusation, and your previous record. A minor charge that is likely to get thrown out should not necessitate your paying good money for a private lawyer. However, do not think that the court system is objective or that "justice is blind." If you bring in Johnny Cochran to defend you on a minor marijuana charge, the district attorney is not going to bother to prosecute. In other words, if you have money, power, or connections, now is the time to use them.

If you feel you have been arrested solely to harass you because you are gay, don't utter a peep to the cops about this. If they have arrested you specifically because you are gay, your protests will only give them further sick amusement. Wait until you are out of jail and then sound every alarm—call the gay press, call the American Civil Liberties Union, call your mother and tell her to spread the word. The only way this type of harassment ever ends is if the light of day shines on it.

Finally, should you find yourself having to spend the night in an orange jumpsuit, remember that it's not the end of the world. Jail is not prison; your fellow incarcerees are either other first-timers awaiting release on Monday morning or minor criminals serving short sentences for minor offenses. Some jails, such as the new one in San Francisco, have with amenities like cable TV and microwaves.

Fag Bashers

There are two kinds of fag bashers: The first are suburban kids who are disturbed and confused about their sexuality and afraid of being gay themselves. These kids are, as a general rule, more likely to taunt, throw bottles, and play "chicken" with gay men than to engage in actual serious violence.

The other kind are hateful to the extreme, full of violent rage and drugs, and they want to take their anger out on somebody. *They* is the operative word here; there is almost no such thing as a fag basher singular. Fag bashers work in packs, at night, and only when they outnumber their prey. If they are aggressive enough to leave their car and come after you, it will only be because they are armed with a weapon—usually not a gun, more likely a baseball bat or knife. Attempting to reason with fag bashers will not work, and begging for mercy will only excite them. Running and shouting as you run is the best defense if you are in good enough shape to outrun a group of overamped teenage boys or young men.

For a while the fashion accessory du jour in the gay community was a whistle; you were to blow it whenever you were threatened and any other gay person in the vicinity would blow his or call for the cops. This accessory is gone now, for the cold fact is that it didn't work. My mother taught me an important lesson in situations like this: "Don't shout 'Help! Police! Murder!' because nobody will open their window. Shout 'Fire!' and people will come running to see."

Defending yourself

Again, the best defense is a good pair of running shoes and 20 minutes a day on the Stairmaster. However, if you find yourself in a position where flight is not an option, there are alternatives, but you will need to be prepared beforehand in order to take advantage of them.

You may never need to worry about fag bashers. I lived in San Francisco for 12 years and was harassed, but I am 6 foot 1 and weigh 200 pounds. It's important to remember that the smaller you are, the more a bully enjoys displaying his power over you—for that is what fag bashers are: bullies. They think like bullies and act like bullies. If you remember your school days, though, you remember that the bully lost his power the day the little kid (who may well have been you) had taken enough judo classes to successfully fight back.

First let it be said that a bashing is not the same as a robbery. Bashers may take your money, but it is not their primary goal. Robbers usually work alone. If a single person comes up to you and has a weapon, or even says he has a weapon, and demands your wallet, give it to him. Most robbers will take the money and run. Let them have it; you can reconstitute your wallet but not your vital organs.

Like being arrested, the most important thing to do when you are confronted with bashers is not to panic. Scope out the situation: How outnumbered are you? Are you with someone who is also prepared for this situation, or is he going to be of no assistance? If you are in a situation where you cannot run, or are with someone who will not make it as fast as you, you will have to defend yourself.

Remember that bashers have been taught that gay men are weak and helpless. You gain the element of surprise the moment you fight back. Since bashers do not operate unless they outnumber you, you are best off attacking the weakest among them and getting through their line there. (Don't forget to start shouting "Fire!" at this point.) Remember that you are not Chuck Norris and this is not a movie; you are not going to beat up three or more (it's always at least three in a pack) thugs and make headlines. Your goal is to escape, not to exact revenge for all the bashings that ever were.

As a precautionary measure you may want to take a basic self-defense course. If you live in a large city, there is probably a gay and lesbian group offering classes taught by a professional. If not, contact your local police department and ask if it offers a self-defense class.

Enrolling in a martial-arts program can be beneficial as well, as disabling one member of a pack with a well-timed, well-placed kick will often send the others running. However, a little knowledge can be a dangerous thing. Chances are good that at least one of the more violent sort of fag-bashers has done some street fighting and will be ready for you; formal martial-arts training cannot prepare you for a dirty fighter with a switchblade. Conversely, don't forget that this is not a gentleman's argument; you are fighting for your life. Gouging out eyes with keys, slashing open bellies with broken bottles, and sending someone into a coma with a well-placed brick are all highly endorsed options here; no jury in the world will send you to jail for defending yourself against a group of attackers.

If you are not physically confident enough to protect yourself this way, pack one of those Sharper Image doodads that feature strobe lights, piercing sound, and Mace. Like animals, the young men in the pack do not like the effects and will usually run. Barring the high-tech approach, Mace is cheap, readily available, and highly effective.

When the police arrive

Chances are that the cavalry won't come over the hill in time to save you. The police are too busy arresting people on alcohol, drug, and morals charges to keep the streets clear of violent criminals.

Even if you get away without a scratch and no blows are exchanged, you need to call the cops. A report needs to be filed so that statistics can be compiled and gay and lesbian agencies can note whether or not a community is becoming a more dangerous or safer place for us to live. It may seem futile to you to provide descriptions of your assailants, especially if the police officer is lackadaisical and tells you, "We'll never catch them anyway," implying that you should save him the bother of filling out the paperwork. Cops are civil servants, and like most bureaucrats they can be lazy. Don't allow it.

Don't expect much sympathy from the officer taking your complaint. Even today cops will sometimes ask if you were engaging in flamboyant behavior or if you made a pass at one of your attackers. Remember that even in enlightened San Francisco, the beat-cop slang for a domestic disturbance is a "bitch got slapped" call. To cops, there is us, and there is them, and you and I are them.

If you have been injured during an attack, seek medical attention at once. This is both for your own good and for the strength of your complaint should your case come to court. There is no way for you to tell when a knock on the head is actually a concussion or if a scratch from a beer bottle is already infected.

Chapter Thirteen

Friends and Roommates

Often, in preparation for or just after coming out, gay men will move to a new city, usually one of the really large ones like New York, San Francisco, Los Angeles, Chicago, or Atlanta. Moving to a new city is scary for anyone, gay or straight. If you are lucky, you have relatives or friends in your new city. If so, do not hesitate to accept their offers to socialize. For most of us, though, starting a new life in a new city means building an almost entirely new circle of intimates.

Friends

This chapter is titled Friends and Roommates. Roommates will come and go, sometimes through a revolving door, but if you are lucky, friends will be with you forever.

Gay men make friends the same way that straight people do—joining social groups, meeting people at work, and meeting people through friends they already have. Gay men also make friends in a way that straight men and women can rarely handle: Oftentimes the men you bring home for sex turn out to be people with whom you have more in common out of bed than in bed and you become friends with them.

Men and women often feel obligated to follow social codes that say you can only be friends if you never, ever have sex and if you do have sex and it's not love, you must part ways. Gay men usually have a more relaxed attitude about sex than straight people. As a consequence we don't automatically load it up with all kinds of baggage.

Remember that sexual love is not the only intimacy available between two men. Sometimes you meet someone and hit it off socially, discovering at the same time that you are sexually attracted to him. If he gives no indication that the sexual attraction is mutual, you can pine away, keeping your secret love alive, hoping that someday, someday... Or you can do the healthy, adult thing and accept that he isn't interested in dating you, but he's as interested in befriending you as you are in befriending him. One of the most mature things you can do is to put aside your unrequited attraction and let the friendship develop, rather than putting all your eggs in the doomed basket of romance. (If he *is* sexually attracted to you, then by all means explore the possibility of becoming more than just friends.)

The younger you are, the faster and more intensely you develop friendships. This is all well and good in high school or college, but once you have come out, you are well-advised to move a little slower and act with a little more caution, especially if you have relocated to a large city. Big cities attract transient people, some of whom have their eye on the quick scam and some of whom are outright sociopaths who develop destructive relationships that are difficult to escape. There is more on this later in this book, in the chapter Getting Scammed, but it's important to mention here as well. Just remember that a friend doesn't ask you to prove your friendship in some financial way. If someone you haven't known very long asks you to loan him money, score drugs for him, or bail him out of jail, think twice before agreeing to "help" him.

Roommates

First off, let it be said that becoming roommates is often the death of friendships. People who get along marvelously visiting each other's homes can suddenly become mortal enemies when they share one. If your college roommate became your best friend, then you are probably going to do well sharing an apartment; otherwise, it's best to think twice before moving in with friends. Roommates in a big city are easily replaced when things go wrong; making friends depends on hard work and good luck, and friends cannot be picked from an agency listing.

Once upon a time there was a magical place; let's call it New York City in the 1950s, or San Francisco in the 1970s, when young gay people could find a cheap place to live in a wonderful, vibrant place full of other gay people. In fact, rent was so cheap that you could work a part-time job and spend the rest of your day working on something creative like painting or dancing or acting or writing.

No more. A studio apartment in San Francisco as of this writing goes for a bare minimum of $900 a month, and that's in the bad part of town. Barring an earthquake, recession, or bursting of the Internet stock bubble, rent will be even higher by the time you read this. As for a studio apartment in Manhattan, they are available, as long as you are willing to live at the top of the island and spend an hour on the subway getting to anything in the heart of the city.

If you want to move to a big city, especially a gay mecca, unless you are earning six figures or are lucky enough to have a generous trust fund, you are going to have to find a roommate situation. At first you may even have to live in the suburbs or in the farther-flung regions of the city. Many people in San Francisco are paying $500 or even $600 for a bedroom in a shared apartment "in town."

First off, you will need to visit the city in question before moving there. If you don't know anybody, this can be expensive, involving transportation costs and a hotel room. If you know anybody at all, throw yourself on his mercy and ask for a few days on his couch while you look for a place to live. Almost nobody grew up in the city, and practically everyone will have had to go through what you are about to go through. If a mutual friend vouches for you, a person will usually accommodate you. If you are very, very lucky, you have someone you can stay with for a few weeks while you find a place. This gives you a local phone number to give to potential roommates and shows that someone trusts you enough (and doesn't find you too irritating) to let you stay with them for that long.

While looking for an apartment, you will also want to find a job—any job. If you do pink-collar work, sign up with several agencies while you are in town and take all their skills tests. If you score well on the tests, get copies. You'll see why in a minute. It will be a huge advantage in your apartment search if you have already lined up a job.

If you are on a low budget, you'll want to pick up the local alternative paper, usually a weekly, and nearly always free. You should also grab a copy of the local gay newspaper. These papers always have at least a few ROOMMATE WANTED ads and are a good place to start. If you do have $50 to $75 to spend, I would strongly recommend you place an ad and peruse the listings of others at a roommate search agency. These agencies give you a questionnaire to fill out, asking how much you are willing to spend, if you have a pet, what part of town you will or won't live in, and sometimes significant personal information. Most larger roommate agencies have now computerized their listings so that you can fill out a query to look for a room in the Castro, cat OK, no more than $500 a month, no smoking or no drugs, etc. Then people looking for roommates may call you if your profile matches their needs.

If you do not have a job but have signed up with a temp agency, you want to show your high scores to potential roommates. It lets you say, "Look, see, I have skills. I am not unemployable." As an out-of-towner you are going to have to provide extra reassurance; the ability to pay two month's rent in advance is an excellent ace in the hole. Of course, you need to be cautious, lest your offer be taken by someone who will skip out with your money.

When you go to look at a place, you will want to meet *all* of your potential roommates. If you like the apartment and things go well with the first roommate, but it's not possible to meet the others at that time, ask for a second visit. Roommate 1 may be eager for you to commit before you meet roommate 2, whom he knows is an unlikable pain in the ass. Remember, no matter now nice people are, they are still strangers to you. Always hold something back, and always remember to exercise a little caution. Almost nobody is who he appears to be on first inspection. Don't feel that he holds all the power, and even if he does—for instance, if you have only one day left to find a place—don't let it show. A display of desperation will usually result in either a statement such as, "I don't think this is going to work, but thanks for dropping by," or a sudden increase in the amount of rent.

The important thing to do with this decision, as with any major decision, is to sleep on it. This means, give yourself until the next day to make a commitment—think about it, talk about it with friends, get some distance and decide if this is really what you want. The last thing you want is a case of buyer's remorse when it comes to a place to live. If someone pressures you to make a decision that instant, treat it like any other hard-sell situation: First, recognize that if he is so hard-pressed that he can't wait a day for your answer, then he is probably desperate to find someone, and his desperation may be a warning sign. Second, realize that in such a situation it is you and not the other party who is operating from the position of power. Call his bluff. Say calmly, "Well, I'm sorry to hear that you have to rent it tonight to either me or Joe Blow because I have to sleep on it. But if Joe changes his mind, give me a call."

Once you have found a roommate situation that looks feasible, the first thing you want to do, before signing any checks or leases, is sit down with your potential roommates and discuss the details. This is something you'll have to do whether you're living with a friend or a stranger. Friend or no, this is a financial entanglement; setting up the rules you will both work with and abide by is the best way to assure a harmonious living arrangement and to avoid unpleasant surprises later on.

As a general rule, rent is split evenly among roommates, although someone with a bigger room or a bedroom with its own bathroom might pay more. Utilities should be split evenly at the beginning; if one person is never home and the other is always home, running the heat or air conditioning at full blast and generating a huge power bill, it might be necessary to renegotiate. It is convenient in more ways than one for everyone to have his own phone.

How you deal with grocery bills will depend on your setup; if your arrangement is more of a communal living space where everyone takes turns cooking meals for everyone else, an even split of the food bill will work out. As a general rule, though, roommates have separate lives, different schedules, and tastes in food that can run from macrobiotic to McDonald's in the same household. It *shouldn't* be necessary for anyone to label their food in the fridge; everybody knows what he's bought, and any friends rummaging through the fridge ought to have sense to ask, "Is this yours?" before digging in. Nobody likes to feel that he needs to hoard food in his bedroom for fear that someone else will eat it. It is a good idea, however, to do a monthly shopping trip for basics like toilet paper and condiments and other household goods, especially if one of the roomies has a membership at Costco or some discount superstore, as the savings gained by purchasing in bulk benefit all the housemates.

You should also discuss the division of household duties. As a general rule, people clean up after themselves in the kitchen, doing their own dishes. It's a good idea to get a board or a calendar on which to assign other duties like cleaning bathrooms, kitchens, vacuuming, and dusting. If it's written down and the responsible person initials it after it's done, nobody can cause unpleasantness by saying, "I did it last week!"

Household order also requires basic rules involving communal space, noise, and visitors. Anybody should be able to have a friend over and spend time with him in the living room, though having multiple visitors or sucking face with someone in the communal space is a little excessive. If you want to throw a party, you need to get the consent of the other roommates and either allow them to join in the planning and invite their own guests or take complete responsibility for cleaning up afterward and repairing any damage your friends inflict on the property of others.

There are times when you want to make your space more comfortable. This can mean painting, installing new blinds or curtains, or purchasing new furniture. In the case of anything nonportable, such as new carpet, the first thing to do is to ask the landlord to pay for it, as you are making an improvement to his property. If you are planning anything major, you should obtain approval from the landlord. You and your roomies may decide that a new couch would be a dream come true but that none of you could afford it separately. Communal property is tricky; if the household breaks up, which it is likely to do eventually, there can be squabbles over who owns the couch. Conversely, if one person buys it and everyone uses it, wear and tear can cause ill will. If you do go in on furniture, make it a cash purchase. The last thing any household needs is another bill to split every month. Additionally, it helps to have a written agreement as to who will get the couch when the household splits up and how much the others should be reimbursed—always less than they put into it, as it will have been used and its value will be lower.

Whether you live with someone or by yourself, you are going to have to deal with the landlord. There are some landlords who are kind, willing to give newcomers a break and who will not jack up the rent every time they can, especially if you are a long-standing tenant with a good payment record. There are also a few people working in the American penal system who aren't sadists, but they're a minority too.

It is important that everything you and your landlord discuss is put in writing. As a roommate, you may wish to be added to the lease, because if the principal tenant vacates and he is the only one on the lease, then the landlord can throw the rest of you out and raise the rent to whatever the market will bear. This is especially important in cities like New York and San Francisco, where living space is scarce and rents are constantly climbing. The downside of being on the lease is that if one of your roommates skips out, you will be responsible for his rent.

If you are in a roommate situation, it is best to have one person in charge of all contact with the landlord. This saves you from situations where the landlord might say, "Well, your roommate Fred said I could come in anytime I want," or worse. This also shows the landlord that you are presenting a united front and that he cannot drive a wedge between the roommates (which has happened in more than one instance in which the landlord wanted to clear everyone out to jack up the rent). Anytime the landlord asks you for something you don't want to grant, such as unrestricted access to your apartment (which is illegal), tell him you will get back to him and then contact your local tenant's right association or, if there isn't one, call the office of your city councilman and ask whom to call in city government for the local ordinances governing renters' rights. These calls are so frequent that the people answering the phone at the councilman's office might have the facts memorized.

Drugs and tricks

These two subjects get their own subheading because they are the cause of more grief in roommate situations than anything else. If you have a drug of choice that you take at home, you are better off informing potential roommates before you move in. More people than you might think either smoke marijuana or have little objection to your smoking it in your bedroom.

The problem comes with the presence of harder drugs. More to the point, the problem you will face one day as the already-established roommate looking for a new person is that most people with drug problems who are looking for a new home do not volunteer that they have a problem. You will only find out about it once they are moved in, because people on hard drugs often fail to pay the rent, having already spent their money on drugs or having lost their job because they were too high to show up once too often. Problems also arise when they or their friends "borrow" items belonging to their roommates to sell for drugs. Additionally, if you are not high and have to spend the weekend with a roommate who is, and who will continue to be until Monday morning, his very presence can wear on your nerves.

As a consequence it is best to state at the initial interview which drugs, if any, will and will not be tolerated in the house.

Tricks are another source of irritation. If roommate 1 has to get up at 6 A.M. every day and roommate 2 stumbles in every night at 2 A.M. with a new "friend" with whom he is laughing, looking for food or Bromo Seltzer in the kitchen, and then spending the rest of the night producing thumps and loud cries—punctuated by trips to the bathroom to throw up—well, roommate 1 is going to be pretty inconvenienced. Rules need to be established about when and how often tricks can be brought home and how much late-night noise is acceptable.

In Conclusion

Some people work like dogs to make the kind of money that will get them their own place as soon as possible; others end up making comfortable salaries but find they enjoy living with others and have roommates until they find lovers. How well it works for you will depend on your temperament and people-management skills.

Talking things out is the most important part of any relationship, personal or business, and in the end a roommate situation is both. Sometimes you may want to schedule a monthly house meeting at which any heretofore unknown gripes can be aired ("Can't you just once put the toilet paper on the roller when you start a new roll?"). Economic necessity doesn't have to mean stress and misery.

Chapter Fourteen

Lovers (and Ex-Lovers)

Chapter 9 of this book provided information on your *first* relationship after coming out. The focus of this chapter is on *serious* relationships. Since I've already written a book on finding Mr. Right, rather than repeat all the information in it, I'll just give you the most important advice—take it slow—followed by a few tips on making relationships work.

When entering into a potentially serious relationship, the most important thing to remember is, as the high school virgin patrol puts it, "true love waits." If you've only known this guy for three months, you don't know him. We all want to be happy as soon as possible, and behind every hasty decision is the nagging fear that what we don't grab today won't be there tomorrow. For purposes of this chapter, though, I will assume that you have thought things through and decided to take the plunge.

That said, here are some things to remember.

The Money Thing

When a serious relationship begins, you are certain that nothing could possibly come between you, especially nothing so crass as money. But the fact is, money is the issue that is *most* likely to cause problems in a serious relationship. Consequently, it is important to set up the financial terms of your relationship before moving in together.

The ideal situation is for the two of you to move into a new place, where you both put your name on the lease (or the deed if you are so rash as to *buy* property with a new love), both put up the same amount of money, and therefore both have a stake in making the arrangement work. Remember, however, that on a lease or a mortgage, if one of the tenants defaults, the other may be liable, depending on local laws. You will want to check into this before renting or buying with someone. If you move into his place or he moves into yours, it's in the best inter-est of the person moving in to get his name on the lease. That way, one lover can't arbitrarily kick the other out, and, as in roommate situa-tions, if one person leaves, the landlord cannot easily toss the other out to make room for a higher-paying tenant.

And as with roommates, remember that when buying items of value, it's important to have a detailed record of who owns what. This is something few couples do, since it's not only "not romantic" but also bespeaks the possibility of a future split. A little cold practicality, however, is nothing compared to fighting over property during a nasty breakup. If you buy a couch together, write down how much each party paid for it; if one of you buys an expensive food processor, write down which of you it was. You may even want to start a rela-tionship book to document your purchases. In the beginning every-thing is "ours" and belongs to "us," and it feels good, and someday you might make a somber ritual of burning that record book. But for now consider it an insurance policy, both against loss of property and dam-age to your nerves.

Some power and phone companies will put both of your names on the bill; others won't. If not, then the one whose name is not on the bill should write the other a check covering his portion of each bill, with a memo notation that that's what it's for. Canceled checks are good evidence if there are financial fights later on and also will help you show that you have paid such a bill regularly, even though your name has not been on it. (This is helpful in establishing good credit.)

As time goes by you may wish to switch off on the accounts, putting one of your names on the phone bill and the other of your names on the power bill, allowing you both to build good credit records.

Fair Distribution of Labor

Your lover is your partner, your best friend, and your soul mate. He is also your roommate, and the same principles apply to getting along with him as with any roommate. If you are lucky, one of you loves to cook but hates cleaning up, while the other is incompetent at the stove but finds washing dishes therapeutic. Chances are, though, that you are both going to have to sacrifice.

In some cases couples find it charming (at least initially) to set up as "husband and wife," where one partner plays the breadwinner and the other plays the homemaker. Over the long term this arrangement is not likely to succeed, as resentments can pile up quickly on both sides—I work all day in this house and you just come home and leave clothes and dishes everywhere for me to pick up; I work all day at the office and now you want me to come home and work some more…

As in any roommate situation, it's best to post a schedule of assigned chores to be checked off so that nobody can accuse the other person of not pulling his weight. Obviously when one of you is sick or out of town, the schedule flies out the window, to be resumed upon that person's returning to town or good health. But barring these exceptions, it's best to stick to some kind of schedule. You may wish to time-share, to have one of you do all the chores one week and none of them the next. The best advice I can give is to experiment and see what works best.

Getting Serious

When I say getting serious I'm talking about something more than moving in together. I'm talking about a financial merger between you and your lover, however tentative or dramatic. This could be starting a joint checking account (separate, of course, from your individual accounts and not taking their place) to buying a house or business together.

When you are about to link your financial future and well-being to another person, it is important to have certain safeguards in place first. These are not just to protect you from your partner's potential financial disasters, accidental or self-inflicted, but to protect you from the American legal system, which does not acknowledge gay partners as spouses under the law. For instance, if your lover becomes ill or incapacitated, you are not automatically his decision maker, as you would be if legally married. In fact, in the eyes of the law, you are no one and can even be kept from visiting him in the hospital. You will not automatically inherit his property if he dies and are not automatically the person who handles his funeral arrangements.

As such, once you are in any financial situation together, you must both have a will drawn up as soon as possible. Otherwise, if he dies, there is no legal guarantee of your property rights unless your name is on everything, and even then there are ways for unscrupulous relatives to screw you.

In addition to a will you should also have a financial power of attorney and a medical power of attorney drawn up so that you and your partner may act as legally married spouses in the event of incapacitation. The financial power of attorney allows you, for instance, to sell the house if you need money to pay medical bills, even though the other owner is in a coma. The medical power of attorney allows both of you to make the important medical decisions, including whether or not to pull the plug.

For more information on creating spousal rights that are not automatically granted to gays as they are to straights, pick up a copy of *Beating the System: The Essential Guide to Personal Finance and Estate Planning for Gay and Lesbian Couples and Individuals* by Theodore Hughes and David Klein.

Sexual Contracts

As a general rule, men like sex. And sex for gay men is much easier to get than it is for straight guys. How two men agree to manage their sexual appetites can be one of the most difficult parts of their relationship.

It is rare to find two men who are inherently monogamous and powerfully attracted to one another. It's more likely that one monogamous man will fall for someone who considers sex to be a recreational activity, as akin to cheating in his heart and mind as picking money up off the sidewalk would be to robbery. If this couple are lucky, the sexual adventurer will find that sex with the monogamist is so good that sex with anybody else suddenly feels like a waste of time. Otherwise, there will need to be some significant give-and-take on both sides to make the relationship work.

The first thing that both parties must do is know their own minds—you cannot negotiate changes in your behavior if you don't see your behavior for what it is. Perhaps your sleeping around is part of your need for approval, and perhaps his monogamy is simple jealousy or fear of losing you to someone better in the sack. You have to be able to articulate your own issues before you can ask the other person to address his and how they clash with yours.

For instance, I was in a relationship with someone who made it clear from the start that he was marriage- and monogamy-minded. I had never been in a monogamous relationship, partly because I had never gotten that far with someone who expected it, and partly because, after 12 years in San Francisco, I had come to see casual sex as more like a diversion than a betrayal. I knew my own mind, however, and was able to say to him at a certain point that I could consider monogamy with him because he was the best sex I'd ever had, and the sacrifice I would be making would not be so extreme as it first seemed. At the same time he decided that the connection between us might be powerful enough that he could settle with me for "monogamy of the spirit." Therefore, we reached an agreement whereby I could have sex with other men on a casual basis, as long as there were no repeat partners that might jeopardize our relationship. We had both decided what was most important to us and were willing to give up things that now seemed less important than they had before we'd met.

The relationship did not fly for reasons unrelated to sex. Had we decided to be monogamous, in time I might have decided I *did* need sex with other men. Or if the relationship lasted longer in its current nonmonogamous state, he might have decided that monogamy of spirit was not enough. Any agreement on a subject like sex is a temporary one. As relationships evolve, people in them grow and change, their needs become different and may well conflict with the other person's needs. If so, this can cause serious problems.

To make a relationship work, sexual terms must be clear from the start and must be tolerable conditions for both parties. There is no point in agreeing to terms you can't abide by in order to "get" a man.

Breaking Up

Breakups can be horrific, with both parties fighting over property and discovering the vast scale of the other's lies and deceit, or they can be amicable, a parting of the ways between two people who have grown apart. Honesty from the start is the best way to avoid a bad breakup.

If you are breaking up, you will be glad to have followed the advice given above, keeping careful records of what belongs to whom. There is usually enough fighting over who's to blame for the breakup without also fighting over who bought the home-theater system. Records are no guarantee of a peaceful distribution of goods, of course, but they significantly diminish the opportunities for squabbling.

Many ex-lovers are or soon become revenge-minded. If this is the case with you and your ex, then it's important to eliminate your entanglements with the ex as quickly as possible. This involves not only taking his name off your powers of attorney but also things as basic as taking him off your account at the video rental store, letting the little lady at the cleaners know it is no longer OK for him to pick up your shirts, informing your landlord that he should not give out your new phone number (which you changed to avoid further nasty calls from the ex) since said ex or his agent may try to call the land-lord and get it using some concocted story.

Remaining friends with an ex is about the most mature thing any-body can do. Remember, though, that even after amicable breakups there are certain natural human responses that will arise when you see him with someone else, especially if he is with someone you might consider to be, at least at first glance, better than you in some way. Staying involved in the life of someone with whom you've had a sig-nificant connection can be a wonderful thing, but it never comes without little stabs of pain, which is probably why most people leave their exes behind entirely.

Resources

For basic information on gay relationships, check out *The Principles: The Gay Man's Guide to Finding (And Keeping) Mr. Right* by Orland Outland (me!).

For a more serious book try *Permanent Partners: Building Gay and Lesbian Relationships That Last* by Betty Berzon.

For information on creating legal protections for you and your partner, read *Beating the System: The Essential Guide to Personal Finance and Estate Planning for Gay and Lesbian Couples and Individuals* by Theodore E, Hughes and David Klein.

Two good Web sites are www.committedpartners.com and www.buddybuddy.com.

Chapter Fifteen

Getting Scammed

Once upon a time it was easy to see a scam artist coming. It was usually an incarcerated gentleman who would place a classified ad in the personals section of a gay paper, looking for "pen pals," who would with any luck offer him a second chance…to steal someone else blind. Or it might have been a street kid whose innocent demeanor concealed a *Primal Fear*-like opportunism.

Gay men were easy targets for scammers because they were far less likely to go to the authorities and report what had happened, out of fear of identifying themselves as gay to the authorities and out of humiliation at having been led down the garden path.

Nowadays the scams and the scammers are more sophisticated; Absolut Vodka is not the only one who's discovered "gay dollars." The best defense against scammers is to pay careful attention to the profile of a scammer I've sketched out below, based on both personal and closely related experiences with the type. If you see these traits in a person you're involved with, it might be best to step back and rethink the relationship.

Blackmail

When the original edition of this book came out, blackmail was still a major threat to gay men. Of course, it continues to be a threat for married or otherwise closeted men or those whose specialized proclivities might land them in hot water or even jail. The advice given previously still stands: If you are out of the closet, you cannot be blackmailed on the basis of your sexuality. If you *are* blackmailed, don't give in—go to the police, or at least to a gay or gay-friendly private investigator who can handle the situation for you. There is no such thing as one-shot blackmail; if you give in once, the blackmailer will assume you will give in again.

The Scammer—A Profile

Before we get into a profile of the scammer, a word about the scammed.

Gay or straight, young or old, now or then, one fact above all: The scam artist preys on lonely and essentially good-hearted people who are eager to please and who probably offer far more than is initially asked for in an effort to bond with this new person. They do not expect sex as a general rule, though they are enormously delighted to get it. They do not expect fawning subservience in return for their help, only a bit of gratitude, not so much for the money as for the emotion behind it.

Scam artists have an unerring nose for this type. They know what the scammee is looking for—affection, attention, interest—in short, love or at least an antidote to loneliness. And in the beginning, scammers provide it in spades. They get you emotionally addicted to them even as they learn your weaknesses through your intimate revelations, which you think are bringing you closer but in reality are only arming him—with the things you feel guilty about or can be made to feel guilty about, with the insecurities you have never entirely overcome, with your sense of shame, and with any other weakness you may have. In short, over time scammers get to know you well enough to play you like a harp. Sometimes they will even excoriate you for doing something *they* are doing behind your back. ("You're cheating on me!") If you find your relationship with someone descending into this kind of emotional abuse and cataloging of your faults, which you can only make up for via more attention and more purchases, you are being scammed.

I used to think I knew a piece of skank when I saw it, that users were people whose desperation made their tactics transparent. In fact, the worst users are well-groomed, articulate, and charming, at least at first. They present a picture of someone worth helping.

I was preyed on shortly after having made the decision to try to help a younger person get started in the city, help I hadn't gotten myself. He was someone I met online; he initiated our first conversation. He lived in the East, having had to move home from San Francisco after an unfortunate roommate experience (which I later realized was probably another scam gone bad). He was smart and funny and seemed enormously grateful to me, his "big bro," for my interest in his life, and the conversations we had that, he said, eased his loneliness and depression about having to move home to the sticks. He complained of deep depression and spoke of suicide. He refused my offer of a plane ticket to San Francisco to visit until finally I offered both the ticket and a place to stay while he looked for his own place. He arrived in San Francisco knowing I was HIV-positive and stating that he couldn't have sex with me, to which I agreed, reiterating that I wanted to help him out, not find a sex toy. His third day here he initiated sex with me, and within several months I was pretty much in his power. He was able to manipulate both my emotions and my wallet.

The important thing to remember about scammers is that in their own minds they are innocent. Theirs is a form of sociopathic behavior enabling them to take advantage of people without remorse, for in scammers' minds there are only two kinds of people: those who have done them wrong and those whose responsibility it is to make it better. The are never at fault for anything; someone else has always driven them to it. They cry and feel pain but only for themselves, never for those they have wounded. They are not responsible for changing the direction of their lives; that has been determined for them, and they are forever helpless babies and therefore someone else's responsibility.

This is not to say that every financially unequal relationship is a scam. A real scam relationship always involves emotional as well as financial abuse; a gay male scammer is usually someone with deep emotional problems, probably including some form of childhood abuse and a huge amount of repressed anger. They come looking for what their fathers (or whoever it is they're angry at) didn't give them, for someone who won't betray them the way their fathers did. But sooner or later in any relationship one person lets the other down a bit, sooner rather than later if the person let down has projected vast needs and expectations on the other. Once you, like their father, have failed to be perfect, the anger and the emotional abuse begin, as the scammer transfers his bottled up rage at his father to the person he has appointed to take his place, the person who is physically there as the father is not, the person the scammer has selected as weak enough to take the mental and sometimes even physical battering he never had the guts to give to the real source of his rage and pain.

Scammers are looking for both affection and a free lunch but in the end will settle for the free lunch. Behind all that rage and pain is a cold calculation. I discovered after I managed to terminate the vampiric relationship in which I'd become entangled, that the person in question had attempted the same tactics on plenty of other people, several of whom I came to know. Those who had seen through him were, oddly enough, the ones who were still fond of him, whereas those of us who had allowed him to use us were angry and bitter. In short, a scammer will try to use you automatically; if he fails, he will respect you and move on; if he succeeds, he will despise you and stay as long as the getting is good.

There is no good end to such a story. After he was gone from my life (in person if not in spirit), I accidentally met someone he hooked up with after me. I found out that all the time that I was raging in pain, angry not just at what he'd done to me but that he'd gotten away with it, he was living even higher on the hog with someone else. In fact, though, what was happening was that he was being used himself by someone a little older who was far better at the game than he was. At the end of that relationship, he was addicted to crystal meth thanks to the constant supply the other man provided, he had lost a frightening amount of weight, and he was broke. No longer in command of the charms that had attracted the better class of usable men, he now found himself doing whatever it took to score more drugs and stay afloat.

Getting Out

Getting out of a scam relationship is a difficult twofold process. First, actual physical separation must occur. This means changing the locks, the phone number, the door code in a security apartment building, and all the other disengagements listed in the previous chapter that are required in any breakup.

It is best to avoid all contact with the scammer after the break; the genius of scammers is their ability to pick not the locks on your door but the locks in your head. By engaging in a dialogue with him, no matter how eager you may be to tell him off, you are only reopening the door, giving him the chance to explain away and seduce and weep to gain your sympathy. The better the scammer, the better he is at knocking down your fresh new defenses. Your best bet is to have a friend intervene; if the scammer calls you, hand the phone to your friend and let *him* tell the bastard off. Scammers work best on lonely people with no defenses and no support system. Once they realize that you are circling the wagons and that the wagons include people who are resistant to their charms, they will move on.

The second phase is to cut the cord inside—that is, to disengage yourself from the emotional hooks he has planted in you. These hooks are not only the ways he managed to get you to react to him, but they are also the ways in which he left you feeling shitty about yourself. After you realize how bad he is and cut the first cord, you will realize that he has spent a significant amount of time rewriting your programming, reducing your self-esteem, getting you accustomed to giving to him as a way of assuaging guilts you never would have felt had he not provoked them. You can find yourself worrying about him, wondering what lies he is telling the new person about you, or stewing in your anger over how stupid you were to fall for what now seems so obvious.

It takes time to let go of this sorrow. You are in mourning for the time you lost loving someone who never cared for you after all, for the ground you lost in your own self-development after he knocked you down a peg or six, for the person you thought you were in love with because you took him at face value until the end. Ending a scam relationship is like a death; the recovery process has the same qualities about it—that feeling of a shock so great it's like being hit by a truck, that feeling of something suddenly sucked out of your life that takes a part of you with it.

After my scam relationship, recovering meant I had to investigate. I needed first and foremost to know why he'd done this to me, lied to me so comprehensively, lied to others about me, why he'd sometimes told not just practical lies to get what he needed but ornate and viciously embellished lies that displayed the contempt he had for the person he was lying about—usually me. I also needed to understand how he had turned me, a reasonably happy but lonely person, into an emotional wreck who had lost, at least temporarily, much, if not all, of my self-esteem. In the end freedom came to me when I heard about his most recent escapade from another man he'd scammed and I was able to coldly and clinically dissect his actions. In the end the remedy for the poisons he left behind came in the form of an antidote I learned to mix myself—he lost his power over me when I understood how that power was acquired and used. I knew that if I did not learn the whys and hows, that it might well happen again.

George, my therapist, once told me he had a test he used to determine whether he would take on a patient. On the patient's first visit he would ask, "What's the problem?" If the answer was something like, "I don't know, my life is a mess, I'm a failure, I can't keep a relationship," then the person was what George calls a "garden-variety neurotic," and he could help. But if that person said, "I never had a chance, my parents fucked me up, and everyone has betrayed me," then George realized he was dealing with a "character disorder," and he could not help, as there is no helping a person convinced that the problem is outside himself. After I fell victim to the scam artist described above, George reminded me that this was a good test to run on new acquaintances to see where they were coming from; scam artists are not garden-variety neurotics, they always have a character disorder.

Chapter Sixteen

Organizing Your Support System

In sunny days of yore, before that durn fool automobile took folks far from their kinfolk, people pretty much counted on their extended family and neighbors to help them out. But once we became mobile we found ourselves living in worlds where we knew nobody, at least at first. Especially as gay people, in many cases cut off from the world of people back home, we were pressed into creating our own extended families.

And the fact is, we got good at it. However cruel and shallow gay men might behave toward each other as strangers, as friends we have not failed the test. During the worst days of the AIDS crisis, we were put through the fire and passed the test. Not only did we stick by our dying friends again and again, no matter the emotional toll, but we also even occasionally managed to make new ones, knowing full well the person we bonded with today might well be dead in a year. Fortunately, the days when AIDS was an automatic death sentence are past. Unfortunately, there is still bigotry in the world, much of which is directed at gays, resulting in the continued need for extended families.

Medical and Mental Health

Gay men have different health needs than straight men. We have different concerns about sexually transmitted diseases, and we have different psychological needs. One of the first things a gay man needs to do is find a good doctor. I would strongly recommend getting a gay doctor if at all possible. If not, I suggest you find a doctor with a large gay practice. Thi⁻ ˙s less a matter of having a sympathetic ear and more a matter of having ᴧn *understanding* one. A gay doctor is likely to have lived through or lived near whatever it is you are experiencing and is more likely to pay closer attention to developments in areas of concern to gay men. Even if you are HIV-negative, do not underestimate the advantage of a gay doctor. For more on this subject, pick up a copy of *Living Well: The Gay Man's Essential Health Guide* by Peter Shalit.

Once you have a doctor, you will want to get two documents. The medical power of attorney is a legally binding document that states specifically who will be responsible for decisions regarding your medical care if you are unable to make them yourself. In our predominantly straight society, the law automatically hands this power to your closest living relative unless you fill out the medical power of attorney. Many gay men have had the rug pulled out from under them, seeing their ailing lovers hospitalized and then seeing that lover swept off to some god-forsaken town by parents or siblings who regard the already stunned companion as the devil and refuse to tell him where his beloved is going. The medical power of attorney places medical decisions in the hands of the person you want to have making them. You will also want to enact a living will, which specifies the conditions under which doctors should or should not pull the plug on you. For more detailed information on powers of attorney and living wills, read *Beating the System: The Essential Guide to Personal Finance and Estate Planning for Gay and Lesbian Couples and Individuals* by Theodore E. Hughes and David Klein.

If you need to seek the services of a mental-health professional, it's best (as it is when seeking general medical assistance) to go to a gay doctor or at the least, a doctor with a large gay practice. A seasoned gay or gay-friendly shrink has definitely seen your problem before and may have even lived it himself. The important thing to remember is that you must find someone whom you can trust explicitly and implicitly. This is not easy; you are looking for someone who will listen and advise but not judge or interfere by phoning "the authorities," be they in the form of your lover, your parents, or the men in white coats.

A Circle of Friends

Although it sounds cold and calculating, an essential part of disaster preparedness is sitting down and making a list of who you are sure you can count on in an emergency. Living in San Francisco, my friend Steve and I, who have now been friends for almost 20 years, made an agreement long ago: In the event of an earthquake we would meet at his friend Michael's house. When the quake of 1989 hit and knocked out power and phones, we did just that, and nothing could have been more comforting during that trying experience than arriving at Michael's house and seeing Steve. Most of us have one person we can count on implicitly, perhaps a lover, perhaps a friend. Consider yourself lucky if you have more than one such person in your life.

Financial disaster is actually harder on friendship than illness or natural disaster. More friendships have ended through the lending of money than anything else. A friendship is an equal relationship, even though one of you may have more money than the other. But once money changes hands as a loan, or one friend's couch becomes another friend's bed, a friendship can become a dependent and sometimes resentful relationship. If you find yourself in a situation where you have nowhere else to turn and you must ask a friend to lend you money, treat it as a business arrangement—and treat the debt as more important than any of your other debts, even those to an official creditor. Your debts to Macy's can be written off by Macy's with little harm to them, whereas unpaid debts to your friends can cause them serious hardship.

Gay at Work

It was not so long ago that the Monday-morning ritual of coworkers rehashing their weekends necessitated a little creative lying. If you painted the house with your lover, you said, "I painted the house." If you spent the weekend at the White Party (a major circuit party in Palm Springs), you said, "I went to Palm Springs." And if you spent the weekend in bed with another man, screwing each other's brains out with the phone unplugged, you said, "I went to visit my aunt."

Today, corporations have vaulted over the heads of politicians in leading the way on gay rights. While there is still the odd old stick who would rather see his company go down in flames than see it headed by a faggot, for the most part our corporate masters don't give a damn what you do away from work. Moreover, those who are truly savvy know their gay employees are quite often more of an asset than their straight ones—we are generally better educated, quicker to learn, eager to please, and not tied down by children who impede our ability to work late or travel. As a recruitment incentive to this marvelous workforce, companies have started to offer domestic-partner benefits equal to those given to legally married straight employees and have not only allowed but also encouraged gay employee groups, often contributing corporate funds to pay some of the group's expenses. If you are not in a large corporation that has enough gay employees to support such a group, you would be well- advised to find a gay professional organization centered around your field.

These groups are an essential part of a support system. The old boy network has managed to keep its place at the top of society for so long because the old boys watch out for their own. The most important thing in qualifying for a job is skills, but the most important thing in *getting* a job is connections. By joining employee and professional groups, you can use the system to your advantage (not to mention the obvious plus of making new friends).

Moreover, if you are working in a company that is not gay-friendly, being out and being a member of such an organization is a powerful defense weapon—it is one of the basic tenets of business that you do not fire someone who does not need to keep the job, because if you do, he will be working for your competitor the next day. And the person who is tapped into a professional network, and thus known and respected by his peers, is not going to be walking the bricks for long.

The Social Whirl

In straight suburban life, communities are built around one's relations with their neighbors and the parents of their children's schoolmates, but gay communities are urban creations, the visible portion of which is built around strips of bars, restaurants, and boutiques. And as childless urbanites, we usually do not know or even care to know our neighbors. For gay people a community is not something you are automatically part of but something you must seek out.

It's funny, but it's often easier to pick up a stranger in a bar, bring him into your home, have intimate relations with him, and toss him out than it is to go to the first meeting of a social group. In a bar everyone's a stranger and you're instantly one of the crowd, whereas in a social club it seems that everyone knows each other, and when you first walk in the door, you are the outsider. Actually, the opposite is true. Nobody in the bar gives a damn if you're there or not; your participation or boycott means nothing. But in a social group your presence is important, and people will welcome you as someone with at least one of the same interests.

If you're shy, arrive five to ten minutes before the scheduled start of the meeting. You'll find people scattered in groups, chatting and catching up, and also a few other solitary adventurers there for their first visit. An efficient organization will have a table set up at the entrance with reading materials relevant to the group that you can busy yourself with while you wait, and a *very* efficient organization will have a welcoming committee and offer new-member orientation.

Resources

For information on gay men and health, check out *Living Well: The Gay Man's Essential Health Guide* by Peter Shalit.

For information on powers of attorney and living wills, pick up a copy of *Beating the System: The Essential Guide to Personal Finance and Estate Planning for Gay and Lesbian Couples and Individuals* by Theodore E, Hughes and David Klein.

Chapter Seventeen

In Conclusion

What can I say? The whole purpose of this book has been to avoid platitudes, moralizing, sermonizing, cheerleading, doomsaying, and any other overarching theme that people seem to reach for in a conclusion. Every life is different, and every coming-out is too. To paraphrase Tolstoy so roughly as to spin him in his grave, "All closeted lives are alike and miserable. Every out, open life is happy in its own way."

When I agreed to write this book, I thought, *What they're basically asking me to do is to write down everything I know about being gay, everything I've learned in the 15 years I've been out.* It's an autobiography of sorts, because I've experienced everything in here firsthand—love, scammers, drugs, social groups, politics, all of it. Not everyone will agree with everything I say. I suspect that many people will wish I'd been more judgmental on the subjects of drugs and bareback sex. I can't be; it's not me. There's a lot I don't like in both the gay or straight worlds, but being gay has taught me more acceptance skills than I would have ever learned otherwise. People used to ask me, "Don't you wish you were straight, if only to be spared all that grief?" Honestly, being gay has brought me certain measures of grief that, yes, I would never have had as a straight man. Even so, I can still say I never wished to be straight, because it never occurred to me that it would be a good thing to be "like everyone else."

I don't know what else to say, other than, "Welcome, congratulations, and good luck!" No matter what else coming out brings you, remember that you are no longer alone, and sometimes that is the most important thing of all.

Appendix One

The Definitive Gay Glossary

Not to brag, but if there is a definitive gay glossary, this better be it. This glossary is a compilation of numerous glossaries from books, the Web, and, of course, the author's own experience. Some things have been left out for practical reasons—it's assumed that you do not need to know all eight French-Canadian phrases to describe homosexual men and acts or every code phrase used at the turn of the century to describe an attractive sailor. Some antiquated phrases have been left in for entertainment purposes, others because they are still in use among the older gay population. Some politically incorrect phrases have been left in as well because, unfortunately, they are still common. Nonetheless, pretty much everything you will need to know to decipher even the most code-laden conversation should be found below.

4-1-1: From the phone number you dial for information, it means gossip, as in "I've been away for a few days. Give me the 4-1-1."

AC/DC: In the 1960s it was used as an adjective describing a person who had sex with either men or women; a bisexual. The term came from the abbreviations for the two types of electrical currents.

Amyl nitrite: Drug used to revive heart patients but also used by some gay men to enhance sexual experience. Also called poppers.

Androgyne: In the early-20th century it was used as a scientific term for an effeminate gay man.

Anilingus: To tongue the anus. See *Rim.*

Attitude: An air of aloof superiority or arrogance, as in "The White Party was hot, but the attitude was a bit much" or "Sure, he's successful, but he has so much attitude."

Auntie: A derogatory term for an older gay man, especially one who is a gossip.

B&D: Bondage and discipline, a form of sexual play in which one partner is tied up and the other (or others) "discipline" him verbally or physically.

Baby dyke: A young or inexperienced lesbian, particularly of high school or college age.

Back room: A dark room designated for sex at the back of a bar or club. During the 1970s gay men's bars initiated the use of back rooms for anonymous sex. In the early 1990s lesbian clubs in New York and San Francisco began to feature back rooms. Some back rooms come equipped with safer-sex items, such as condoms and latex gloves, but others do not. In many cities back rooms are back in vogue and usually dark enough for unsafe sex to go on as in the '70s.

Banana queen: Someone who has a fetish for a curved penis.

Bar biography: Revisionist family or personal history; a false and inflated description of oneself or history, as in "He's a waiter, but according to his bar biography he's a successful actor." Anyone looking to locate lost members of the Russian imperial family would do well to start in gay bars.

Bareback fucking: Screwing without using condoms. Also known as raw sex. When escorts or people in personal ads want to advertise their willingness to fuck bareback, the code words used are often *adventurous, uninhibited,* or *open to most scenes.*

Basket: A man's crotch, particularly the eye-catching bulging of his genitals in tight pants.

Bashing: Physical assault of lesbians and gay men because of sexual orientation. Also commonly called queer bashing, gay bashing, and fag bashing.

Baths, Bathhouse: Members-only (meaning you pay a fee to "become a member" and enter) establishments built around a set of showers, hot tubs, and steam rooms, often also with small gyms and small private rooms available for men to rest or, more likely, have sex in. Baths often have group-sex areas and glory holes for cock sucking. Some provide safe-sex education to populations that would otherwise not be exposed to it, such as the many married or closeted gay men who are afraid to go to gay bars or have anything but anonymous encounters. Most baths were closed during the AIDS hysteria of the '80s, which only pushed horny men back out into parks and alleys where condoms, showers, and other basic sanitation wasn't available.

Bear: A hairy man, usually with a beard and almost always with some type of facial hair, usually also big and heavy, dressed in a more rural or blue-collar version of the clone uniform. See the chapter on subcultures for more.

Beard: A person of the opposite sex, either heterosexual or homosexual, who knowingly or unknowingly dates or marries a closeted lesbian or gay man to provide that person with a heterosexual "disguise," usually for family or career purposes. Closeted gay actors often show up at awards ceremonies with a beard.

Bent: British slang for *gay*.

Berdache: In approximately 130 American-Indian cultures this term referred to men or women who were unable or unwilling to fit into the role assigned to their gender. The word is a French one meaning "slave boy."

Bestiality: Interspecies sex in which one partner is human.

b.f.: "Boyfriend."

Bi: Bisexual; a person who is sexually attracted to and has emotional relationships with both women and men.

Black triangle: A symbol in the shape of an inverted triangle that was adopted by lesbian culture in remembrance of the lesbians who were killed by the Nazis in Europe.

Blow job: A sex act in which one sucks or licks a man's cock, usually until he has an orgasm. (Why the word *blow* is used when one actually sucks is lost to history).

Bondage: See *B&D*.

Boner: An erect penis; a hard-on.

Booty bump: Drugs, usually crystal meth, mixed with water and injected up a person's ass.

Boston marriage: A relationship in which female partners live together without necessarily having a sexual relationship. Can also refer to a pair of gay men for whom sex is no longer a part of their relationship.

Bottom: The one sucking a penis or getting fucked during sex. He is still called the bottom even if he positions himself above his partner or if he is the one doing most of the moving. Some people are bottoms for the duration of a certain act; others advertise themselves as bottoms meaning they do not expect genital reciprocation during sex.

Boy: A vague and fluffy term in gay culture, generally referring to an 18- to 25-year-old male, still possessed of a certain youthful glow and quite possibly even a shred of innocence. However, it can also refer to a sex role, especially in S/M, where the master can be 18 and his boy can be upward of 90.

Boy toy: A bit more definitive than *boy*, a boy toy is young, probably 18 to 23 years old, and a dance-club habitué who keeps up with the latest hair, clothing, and body fashions. He may or may not be able to support his habits without help from a "patron," but if he needs one, he is usually hot enough that he can find one only slightly older than himself who is not undesirable.

Boyfriend: Usually something between a friend and a lover, although many longtime companions under the age of 40 prefer to stick with the label of *boyfriend* even though they have lived together for years, less out of fear of commitment than out of distaste for the available alternatives like the dry, businesslike *partner* or the secretive, furtive *lover*.

Breeder: A disparaging term for a heterosexual.

Brown: Sometimes a reference to anal sex but more often a reference to someone into feces as a part of sex. See *Scat*.

Buffet flat: An after-hours partying spot in Harlem of the 1920s, usually in someone's apartment, which was a common place for African-American lesbians and gay men to socialize. *Buffet* referred to a smorgasbord of sexual possibilities—straight, gay, groups, etc.

Buggery: An archaic term for anal sex that dates back to the Middle Ages in Europe.

Bump: A single line or hit of a powdered drug such as crystal, cocaine, or special K.

Butch: A lesbian who prefers masculine dress, style, expression, or identity; a gay man who is traditionally virile or masculine in speech, dress, and sexual behavior.

Butch it up: To try to act masculine.

Camp: Exaggerated gestures, styles, and emotions, effeminate and theatrically overblown. "Miss Mary Girlfriend, she is too tired to work it anymore, and that dress is so over I could die!" A classic definition is "a style of humor based on exaggeration, artifice, and androgyny." Within the gay community the term most often refers to gay men assuming an exaggerated feminine manner in order to entertain (mostly for heterosexuals who find masculine homosexuality and its implied sexual power threatening). In camp, the exchange of gay men's names for women's is also common—George becomes Georgette; Robert becomes Roberta, etc. There are also standard camp names by which gay men refer to each other, like Mary or, especially among African-American gay men, Miss Thing. A highbrow approach to the subject can be found in Susan Sontag's classic essay "Notes on Camp."

Catamite: Originally, since the 1500s, it meant a young boy or man kept by an older man for sexual purposes. Now it refers to any male bottom in anal sex, although the phrase is not in common usage.

Cherry Grove: A summer beach resort community on Fire Island founded in the late-19th century. Its inhabitants are predominantly gay and wealthy East Coasters.

Chicken: A young gay man, usually 18 or younger, usually slender and smooth.

Chicken hawk: Derogatory slang for an older gay man who pursues young boys or young men. Usually refers to a man taking advantage of a young runaway's economic hardship for his own sexual gratification.

Circle jerk: Group masturbation or jerking off.

Circuit: The annual string of big dance parties in various locations, including the White Party, Black Party, Hotlanta, and the former GMHC Morning Party. See the Subcultures chapter for more.

Circuit queen: One who does, or even lives for, the circuit.

Clone: Originally, the word *clone* referred to a gay man who sports an outfit and grooming traits that were made popular in New York and San Francisco in the 1970s, including short hair, a mustache, good muscle definition, a flannel shirt, and Levi's. In the early 1990s, *Queer Week* magazine shook up youngster's certainties that they were so different from the clones by defining the new clone look—very short hair with long sideburns, a clean-shaven face or "interesting" facial hair, a lean body, a white T-shirt (probably with an ACT UP logo), Levi's, and Doc Marten boots. Every gay generation produces its own clone look, morphing from the last generation's; today's is a natural outgrowth of economic change—the minimalism of the early-'90s recession chic-grunge look remains, only now it's retailed through Banana Republic in designer neutrals with a high-sheen finish at high-end prices, and Abercrombie & Fitch has replaced Gap and Urban Outfitters in the casual department.

Closet queen: A gay man who keeps his homosexuality a secret from friends, family, and coworkers.

Coming out: What this book is all about; to acknowledge one's homosexuality, to oneself and to others, most often a public declaration of being lesbian or gay.

Coming-out story: An individual's personal story, usually a mix of humor and pathos, about realizing he is gay for the first time, having gay sex for the first time, telling family, friends, or colleagues he is gay, or being discovered involuntarily as gay by family, friends, or colleagues.

Control queen: Someone who needs to have a say in everything or to take charge of every situation.

Condom: Latex shield placed over a penis or sex toy during penetration. Slang terms include *life jacket, rubber, johnson cover, billet-doux, prophylactic, love glove, sleeve, wiener wrap, raincoat, sombrero, pocket pal, rubber duckie, home hood, umbrella.*

Cornhole: Slang for anal sex.

Crack: More likely to refer to crystal meth in gay culture than to crack cocaine, which is referred to if ever as "crack crack."

Crime against nature: Term used by religious fundamentalists to describe homosexuality; taken from wording in the Old Testament. Homosexual sex is described as being "against nature" because it does not lead to the procreation of children, the supposed "natural" use of sexual organs. See *Leviticus*.

Cross-dressing: The practice of dressing in clothes traditionally assigned to the opposite gender; often called transvestism or drag.

Cruise, Cruising: To look for sexual partners; to flirt with the intention of finding a sexual partner. A certain sexual intent in a look someone else gives you that cannot be described in words and does not need to be.

Crystal: Crystal methamphetamine; slang terms include *Tina, Crissy, ice, glass, crack*. Addictive stimulant snorted, smoked, injected, or booty bumped. Gives increased energy, sense of well-being, joy. After addiction sets in, none of these feelings is possible without ever-increasing daily use of the drug.

Cybersex: The computer equivalent of phone sex, only conducted on the Internet via keyboard rather than telephone receiver.

Daisy chain: Three or more men engaged in simultaneous anal sex.

Dairy queen: Likes to suck nipples, almost, if not completely to, the exclusion of other sexual activity.

Date: One definition calls it "someone you begin an evening with, though may not end the evening with." Also used as hustler or escort slang for tricks or johns.

For days: Camp slang meaning many or large, as in "That guy has arms for days."

Dish: Gossip, hearsay, or buzz; often bad or scandalous news.

Domestic partnership: An official recognition of partners (either homosexual or heterosexual) who are not legally married but who cohabitate and share a committed spousal relationship.

Don't go there: A command, or a warning, often humorous, meaning "don't start talking about that."

Don't ask, don't tell: Used to describe U.S. military policy adopted in 1993 to allow gays and lesbians to serve in the military if they keep their sexual orientation a secret and do not engage in gay sex. More gay men and lesbians have been discharged annually since this policy was enacted than were discharged before it.

Drag: In the abstract it refers to clothing, hair, and other affectations of a temporarily adopted style that's not really your own, which could be chosen like biker drag, leather drag, cowboy drag, or imposed on you, like office drag.

Drag balls: Used since the early-20th century in Harlem, this term refers to cross-dressing fashion and dance competitions attended by both straight and gay people; made famous by Madonna's "Vogue" video and the film *Paris Is Burning*.

Drag queen: A man who dresses in women's clothing and affects women's mannerisms, sometimes only in evenings for performances, though sometimes on a semipermanent basis. Different from transvestites in that drag queens never really look like women.

Drama: Big emotional personal turmoil, such as a relationship breaking up or a disastrous dinner party; the makings of good gossip.

Drama queen: Someone who lives to either relate (or create) drama.

Dutch boy: Men, gay or straight, who like to hang around dykes.

Earring: In the 1970s and 1980s it was thought by gays and straights that wearing a stud or post earring in the left ear was code for being gay. Archaic now that the straightest boys in town have multiple earrings on both sides.

Ecstasy, E, X, Buying a vowel: Designer hallucinogenic drug. See the chapter on drugs.

Enema: Squirting water or a prepared mixture into the anus to clean it out thoroughly in preparation for anal sex.

Exhibitionist: Somebody who likes others to watch when he has sex or who likes displaying himself without a partner.

Fag hag: A straight woman who spends an inordinate amount of her time with gay men (often considered a derisive term).

Fag, Faggot: Some people believe that the use of the epithet *faggot* for a gay man began as far back as the 14th century, with the medieval practice of executing homosexuals by burning them at the stake using bundles of sticks, or faggots. In the 1500s the term *faggot* also referred to a disagreeable or outcast woman and may have been extended to include gay men, who were equated with women. Other possible origins of the term include the early 20th–century British slang for a cigarette, a *fag*, since at that time smoking anything other than a cigar was considered effeminate. British slang also included *fagging*, the system in public schools (what we call private schools) in which older boys were the masters of younger boys, who "fagged" for them— menial labor and sometimes sexual service as well.

Family: Used as an adjective for a possibly gay person, as in "Is he family?"

Faygeleh: Yiddish expression for gay; from the word for bird. Derogatory.

Felch: To suck semen from the anus

Fellatio: A blow job.

Female impersonator: A man who dresses in women's clothing and affects women's mannerisms for the purpose of public entertainment, usually impersonating a celebrity such as Judy Garland, Barbra Streisand, Bette Davis, or some other gay icon. Female impersonators are not always gay.

Fem: A derogatory term for an effeminate gay male or a nonderogatory term for the more feminine partner in a lesbian relationship (as opposed to the "butch" partner).

Fetish: Overpowering attraction for some particular aspect of a person or style of dress, such as feet or leather.

Fierce: Gay African-American slang meaning "great"; the highest compliment that can be paid by or to a queen—a truly remarkable dance-music singer is a "fierce house diva."

Fire Island: A barrier island off the coast of Long Island, New York, known for its two gay beach resorts, Cherry Grove and Fire Island Pines.

Fish: Gay male slang for a woman; derogatory. Derived from the alleged smell of a vagina.

Fist-fuck: To put your entire hand, rubber gloved during safe sex, into the anus of another. The hand is held in a cone shape to insert. A dangerous activity not to be performed with a stranger, especially as the bottom.

French active, Fr/a: A person who gives blow jobs while his partner kicks back and enjoys.

French passive, Fr/p: The other guy.

French embassy: Obscure slang for any location, especially a gym or YMCA, where gay sex is readily available.

Friend of Dorothy's: Archaic; anyone gay. The same as "he is family." This term has roots in older gay men's obsession with Judy Garland, who played Dorothy in *The Wizard of Oz*.

Frottage: The ultimate safe sex. Rubbing bodies together, perhaps with some oil, from the French word *frotter*, meaning "to rub."

Flaming: Flamboyantly queeny.

Flor: Spanish slang for a gay man; in English translation it means "flower."

Fluffer: In gay porn this is the person whose job it is to make sure the stars are "up" for their parts.

Freedom rings: Necklace created by David Spada, a New York designer, composed of anodized aluminum rings in the colors of the rainbow and worn loose on a chain. Freedom rings—to some signifying gay pride and unity, to others signifying a crass commercialization of a civil rights struggle—have since been incorporated into numerous kinds of gay jewelry, including earrings, rings, bracelets, and other tchochkes.

Fruit fly: See *Fag hag*.

Fuck buddy: A casual sex partner, usually a friend with whom one has infrequent sex without emotional commitment. An invaluable asset in any single gay man's life.

Fudgepacker: Derogatory heterosexual slang for the top in anal sex. Usually used in the same breath as "Hershey highway," probably by someone who's dying to get fucked but never will be.

Gag reflex: What happens when most men attempt to get another man's penis past the back of their mouth and down into the throat. According to historian Allan Berube, as a screening test employed by Army doctors during World War II to try to detect homosexual men in the ranks, a tongue depressor was inserted deep into a soldier's throat to see if he gagged. If he didn't, it was considered likely that he was accustomed to performing fellatio.

Gaydar: The uncanny and seemingly innate ability lesbians and gay men have to recognize and detect one another; from *gay* and *radar*. A skill now harder to master as gay and straight young people look and act increasingly similar.

Genderfuck: Gender-bending with an attitude; drag that makes a sociopolitical statement. A gender bender is one who blurs gender lines rather than adopting the accepted mannerisms of the opposite sex.

Get her!: Disbelievingly contemptuous shock at another's preposterous behavior.

Girl, Girlfriend: In camp, especially among African-American gay men, used for a fellow gay man who is a close friend and confidant.

Glory hole: A hole drilled through the partition between two stalls in a men's public toilet, or between two booths in an adult bookstore, to allow a penis to be put through for anonymous sex, or to allow for voyeurism.

Golden shower: Urinating on another man during sex play. See *Water sports.*

Granola lesbian: A wholesome, health-conscious lesbian, often irritatingly didactic on the subjects of red meat and white sugar. Sometimes referred to as a "crunchy dyke." Often refers to a whole hard-left politic and lifestyle in addition to dietary habits.

Green queen: Someone who prefers sex outdoors.

Green suit: Archaic; in the early-20th century, wearing a green suit was considered a bold statement of homosexuality. A "green and yellow fellow" in the mid 1900s meant a gay man.

Greek active, Gr/a: The active partner in anal sex; the one who fucks the other's ass. The top is still called active even if he lies still and the guy he is screwing does all the work.

Greek passive, Gr/p: The passive partner in anal sex; the one being fucked.

Guiche: A piercing—a small weight or ring worn in the perineum. (Yes, there is a definition of *perineum.*)

Grower not a shower: A man whose penis when flaccid may not be impressive but which when fully erect is a thing of beauty and a joy forever.

Guppies: Gay yuppies.

Gym bunny, Gymbot: A man whose life revolves around the gym.

Hankie: By wearing different colored hankies, in either the left or right rear hip pocket, a gay man in the 1970s could tell others exactly what sorts of sexual activities he enjoyed. It is not used as much as it was; however, the canonical list is appended to this book.

Harvard style: Screwing by inserting the penis between the thighs of another guy. See *Princeton rub.*

Helium heels: Used as adjective or nickname for a total bottom—i.e., "The minute he lies down, his heels are up in the air."

Heterosexual privilege: Loosely defined, it means the "special rights" of nongay people to present an unedited version of their weekend activities to their coworkers, to place photos of their loved ones on their office desks, and to kiss in any public space, all without fear of repercussions.

Homoerotic: An erotic presentation or situation that is suggestively homosexual in nature, even though its participants may be unaware of it, such as patting a fellow football player on the ass or living on a submarine for six months at a time.

Homophobe: A hater of gay people; one who is actively homophobic.

Homophile: An early-20th century word for homosexuals.

Homosexual panic: Conscious fear of one's own possible homosexuality, often used as a legal defense when a straight man kills a gay man, the reason being the gay man's (undoubted) advances on the straight man.

House: A close-knit group of gay friends, transvestites, and transsexuals, bonded for support, community, camaraderie, and protection, usually in the African-American community. Often structured and ruled by a mother; often named after its founder, such as the house of LaBeija.

House mother: In the Harlem house drag culture, the authority figure or "mother" who heads or oversees the "children" of the "family."

Humpy: Adjective for a gay man who is good-looking and sexually desirable.

Hung, Well hung: Having a big dick.

HWP: "Height-weight proportionate"; a personals ad acronym indicating that one need not be buff to answer the ad, but one must not be officially overweight.

In the life: In the African-American gay community it is the term commonly used for being gay.

Invert: Pseudoscientific term used by psychologists and doctors from the late-19th century until the 1940s for a lesbian or gay man; homosexuality was referred to an inversion or the inverted sexual instinct.

K-hole: A state of disorientation resulting from overindulgence in Ketamine. Occasionally results in irreversible coma. See the chapter on drugs.

Kinsey 6: One whose sexual experience and identification is exclusively homosexual. The Kinsey scale goes from 1, 100% heterosexual with no homosexual experiences or desires, to 6, the polar opposite.

Lambda: An international symbol of homosexuality, the lambda is the 11th letter of the Greek alphabet and has been a symbol of the gay rights movement since 1970.

Leather queen: See *See Tarzan, hear Jane.*

Lesbian: A female homosexual. The term literally means a resident of the Greek island of Lesbos, where the ancient lyric poet Sappho lived. Her verse often celebrated love between women.

Lesbian bed death: The lack of sex that may occur when lesbians are in a long-term relationship.

Library: Antiquated; an adult bookstore.

Leviticus: The book in the Old Testament from which passages are used by the Christian right to justify homophobia and anti-gay discrimination. In addition to condemning a man for lying with a man as with a woman, Leviticus also enjoins the faithful from cutting their hair or beards, getting tattoos, eating anything they grow on their land for four years (the first three years' worth being discarded and the fourth year's crop being given in offering to the Lord). Moreover, Leviticus also considers adultery a crime punishable by death—meaning all those divorced and remarried Republican congressmen who passed the Defense of Marriage Act are as guilty of violating the laws of Leviticus as any gay man.

Lipstick lesbian: A lesbian who is unable to embrace traditional lesbian "butchness" when confronted with a rack of lovely new Chanel suits.

Lollipop stop: A highway rest stop used by gay men for cruising.

Love that dares not speak its name: Phrase used by poet Lord Alfred Douglas (lover of Oscar Wilde) for homosexual love and desire. Only known today because Armistead Maupin recoined it, saying of San Francisco that it was "a city where the love that dares not speak its name never shuts up."

Lover: A longtime companion, a partner, or someone you expect to spend the rest of your life with.

LTR: "Long-term relationship." Not necessarily forever but more than a year.

Lucky Pierre: The third in a three-way with two lovers or boyfriends.

Mariposa: Spanish slang for a gay man; in English translation it means "butterfly."

Maricon: Spanish slang for a gay man; roughly equivalent to *faggot*.

Mary: A campy form of address, as in "Mary! Did I see you making out with that hot boy of Fred's the other night?"

Master: The dominant partner in an S/M relationship.

Mattachine Society: A gay organization founded in Los Angeles in the early 1950s that advocated acceptance and understanding of gays and equal rights for gays.

Meat rack: Traditionally it refers to an outdoor spot where gay men congregate for casual public sex; in general usage it is any bar or street corner where it's easy to get laid.

Ménage à trois: Sexual encounter involving three partners.

Milk?: Word used to stop someone who is being catty.

Miss Thing: A title or form of address for a nelly, flamboyant, or haughty gay man, as in "Miss Thing is working my last nerve."

Mitten queen: Likes to masturbate others.

Molly: Oldest-known British slang term for a gay man.

MOMD: "Man of my dreams."

Moumoune: French-Canadian for a gay man.

Nancy, Nance: A gay man; taken from 19th-century British slang for buttocks; also called Nancy-boy.

Napkin ring: A cock ring.

NAWW: "Not a well woman"; camp vernacular used to describe someone mentally unstable.

Nellie, Nelly: Outrageously effeminate or silly.

On fire: Either derogatory, as in flaming, or complimentary, as in equivalent to fierce.

Only good for the "three gets": Good only for quick, unemotional sex, having no other redeeming value—get off, get dressed, get out.

Opera queen: Anything from a gay man who enjoys opera to a swooningly aesthetic opera fanatic completely out of touch with reality and unable to connect with any but the most overacted silent-movie emotions.

Orgy: Any group sex involving five or more guys. Three people is a threesome, four people is a foursome, and then they run out of *somes* and start calling it an orgy.

Outing: The controversial practice of publicly revealing the sexual orientation of gay celebrities or public figures against their wishes; now usually limited to those profiting off the gay community or merchandising a gay flamboyance while themselves refusing to discuss their sexuality.

Pansy: Used since the early-20th century to refer to a gay man.

Pansy raid: Archaic; a police raid on a gay bar.

Pedophile: An adult who is driven to perform sexual activity with children. However, the term is often used for an adult who likes sex with sexually mature teenagers, particularly those not at the legal age of consent.

Perineum: The crotch area between your balls and your asshole.

Phone sex: Sexual play over the telephone, usually involving mutual masturbation and a $2-per-minute charge.

Piercing: Cuts made in the body through which jewelry is inserted. On gay men this usually involves ears, nipples, navels (if you have a flat stomach), penises (a penis piercing is called a Prince Albert), and perineums.

Pink triangle: A symbol of the gay rights movement that is always with point facing down; originated in Nazi concentration camps as the symbol worn by those interred and killed for being gay.

Polari: A gay British slang that is so complicated it has spawned numerous dissertations. Brought into gay American awareness only through Morrissey's song "Polari Palaver."

Poppers: Originally it referred to amyl nitrate, but over-the-counter sale of amyl nitrate was banned by federal law; now it usually refers to butyl nitrate, a volatile liquid sold as "room deodorizer" or "VCR head cleaner." When inhaled, amyl causes increased heart rate and blood pressure, disorientation, and can enhance sexual pleasure. Amyl nitrate is known to be a relatively safe drug, but none of the analogs have been tested for safety. They are suspected to be immune-system suppressors.

Post-op: A person who has recently undergone sex-reassignment surgery and has changed his birth sex. See *Transsexual.*

Pre-op: A person preparing for sex-reassignment surgery by taking hormones and receiving counseling.

Precome: Clear fluid produced in the prostate and ejected by a man's penis before ejaculation.

Prince Albert: A metal ring worn through a piercing on the underside of the tip of the penis.

Princeton rub: Screwing by inserting the penis between the thighs of another guy. See *Harvard style.*

Prostate: The gland that creates the precome fluids. It swells up and feels like a golf ball when you have an orgasm. It is inside the body between the asshole and the belly button. Having it hit just right is what makes you scream when you get fucked.

Pushing box: Arranging oneself to accentuate one's natural gifts or compensating with artificial devices (such as socks) for what nature failed to provide.

PWA: "Person living with AIDS."

Queen: A flamboyant, nelly gay man.

Queer: Since the early-20th century this has been used as a derogatory term for *homosexual.* Since the early 1990s it has been used an alternative to *gay* and *lesbian. Queer* blurs both gender and sexual orientation and indicates a more hard-left political slant than *gay.*

Quilt, the: A huge commemorative quilt made up of more than 2,000 6-by-3-foot panels. Each panel is a memorial to at least one person who has died of AIDS complications.

Rainbow flag: Designed in 1978 in San Francisco by artist Gilbert Baker as a symbol of lesbian and gay pride. Originally a symbol of the 1978 San Francisco Gay Freedom Parade representing the diversity of the gay community, the rainbow and rainbow flag have been adopted as symbols of the entire gay movement, as well as a merchandiser's wet dream, as gay people can be sold a new piece of virtually anything they already own if the new item has the rainbow palette on it.

Read: Camp slang meaning to degrade someone with a torrent of usually true statements, often in front of other people; a major series of insults, as in "Get out your library card; I'm about to give this girl a serious reading."

Red necktie: In the early-20th century, wearing a red necktie was a code by which gay men could identify one another. What that would make of Washington, D.C., today is left to your imagination.

Red ribbon: A loop of ribbon fastened to the lapel or shirt with a small safety pin indicating AIDS awareness.

Rent parties: In 1920s Harlem this referred to house parties at which guests paid a fee to help their host raise money for the rent. Usually a mix of heterosexuals and homosexuals, rent parties were a safe way for African-American lesbians and gay men to socialize away from speakeasies.

Rice queen: A nelly gay Asian or a white admirer of Asian men.

Rim: To tongue the anus, and possibly to insert the tongue into the anus; also called anilingus. Rimming is also called a rim job. This is considered unsafe as it can pass pinworms, amoebas, intestinal parasites, hepatitis, and almost any other disease the lickee is carrying.

Rough trade: An ostensibly heterosexual man who seeks out sex with gay men, either as the top in anal sex or who gets a blow job, who may or may not become violent at the end of the sexual encounter.

Roles, Role Playing: Opposite functions played out by sexual partners, such as top or bottom, or fantasy characters played by sexual partners in a scene, such coach-jock, dad-son, etc.

ROFL: "Rolling on the floor laughing." Used in online chat.

S/M: Sadomasochism. A form of consensual sexual play involving the exploration of power and sometimes pain.

S&M bar: Stand and model bar; a bar frequented by pretty boys where everyone poses for everyone else but nobody actually speaks, let alone gets laid.

Safe sex: Sexual relations in which the participants take precautions to prevent the spread of sexually transmitted diseases, particularly HIV. See the chapter on sex.

Safer sex: An array of sexual practices that may decrease the risk of HIV infection by preventing the transmission of bodily fluids during sex. Not as guaranteed safe as safe sex but better than unsafe sex.

Scat: Sexual activity involving feces

See Tarzan, hear Jane: A man who appears butch until he speaks, at which time a screaming queen rips off the crewcut to reveal a wig.

Sex reassignment: The surgical alteration of a person's birth sex. See *Transsexual*.

Sexual orientation: Sexual identification, commonly defined as homosexual, heterosexual, or bisexual depending on a person's sexual relationships or affinity.

Shade: Camp slang meaning attitude. When you are throwing shade you are so big and important that you overshadow everyone else.

Shrimping: Toe sucking.

Significant other: A term for boyfriend, lover, or partner that avoids the baggage those words can carry. A term that originated with gays and has been adopted by straight people.

Sings in the choir: Another phrase meaning someone is gay.

Sisters: See *Girl, Girlfriend.*

Sixty-nine: Simultaneous fellatio, belly to belly, head to tail. Also applies to a similar position for heterosexual couples.

Size queen: A gay man who prefers large penises.

Smooth: Absent of or shaved of all body hair.

Snap: An African-American gay signifier; snapping of fingers used to punctuate; *snaps* are clever put-downs of the "Your mamma is so fat" variety.

Snow queen: In Caucasian usage it refers to a gay man addicted to cocaine; in African-American usage it refers to a black man who only dates white men.

Sodomy: Classically defined as any penetrative sexual act that cannot lead to procreation, including oral or anal sex between a man and woman, or any penetrative sex between two men or any sex at all between two women.

Stonewall rebellion: The riots that took place on the streets of Greenwich Village in New York City beginning early in the morning of June 28, 1969 (the day Judy Garland was buried), when patrons of a gay bar called the Stonewall Inn fought back against a police raid of the bar. Stonewall has come to signal the birth of the modern lesbian and gay rights movement. The reason many gay pride celebrations take place the last Sunday of each June or the Sunday closest to the original date.

Sugar daddy: An older man of means who supports a younger man of motives.

Swish: An effeminate gay man; for gay men it means to act in a traditionally feminine way by swinging one's hips when walking.

Tea dance: Originally an Edwardian social occasion that allowed ladies yet another opportunity to change clothes that day. As a gay tradition, an afternoon dance often outside and usually on a Sunday; started at the Blue Whale on Fire Island in 1966. Usually the place to find people who have been dancing nonstop since Friday night.

Tearoom: Any public toilet that becomes a popular spot for anonymous sex between gay men.

Third sex: A name given in Weimar Germany to homosexuals.

Tired: Boring or out of fashion; something or someone whose 15 minutes are up.

To die for: Fabulous.

Top: In sex it refers to one who fucks or gets sucked.

Transvestite, TV: A person who constantly dresses in the clothes of and assumes the gender expression of the opposite sex.

Transsexual, TS: A person who has undergone or is preparing to undergo sex-reassignment surgery.

Trade: A heterosexually identified man who seeks out sex with gay men, either as the top in anal sex or receiving fellatio; it also refers to a hustler or the state of being a hustler.

Transgender: An umbrella term for anyone blurring the lines of traditional gender expression, including transvestites, transsexuals, drag queens and kings, and cross-dressers.

Trick: A casual sexual partner; a person with who one has a brief sexual encounter. In the hustler world it means someone who pays money for sex.

Troll: An older man who is unattractive less for his physical appearance than for his shameless leering and his inability to take no for an answer.

Twirled: High on drugs.

Twinkie, Twink: A young gay man who is sexually desirable for his handsome looks or build, his intellect being irrelevant. Derived from Hostess Twinkie: one who is sweet, golden, cream-filled, and ready to eat.

Uncut: Uncircumcised.

Undinism: Medical term for someone who enjoys urinating on or being urinated on.

Vanilla sex: Conventional sex, with the connotation of boring, that does not incorporate any S/M, fantasy, or any inventive sexual play. The gay version of the missionary position.

Versatile: Likes to both fuck and get fucked. Often used by 100% bottoms who don't want to admit it.

Vibrator: A battery-powered latex-covered penis-shaped device that vibrates. It can be inserted in the anus to stimulate the prostate gland.

Vogue, Voguing: From the fashion magazine; a dance form consisting of a series of precise, measured, and stylized poses like those a model might affect on a fashion runway; often competitively against other voguers. Originated in black gay house culture and brought to the straight world by Madonna's "Vogue" video.

Wanna-be: Anyone trying too hard to look like he belongs in a subculture when he obviously doesn't.

Water sports: Any sex play involving urination, including golden showers or piss enemas, in which a man pisses up another man's ass, usually when both are high on crystal, making it a powerful booty bump.

Work: A flexible word. One can work the room, or work it, as in working the runway, as in, "You better work," as singer RuPaul enjoins listeners in "Supermodel." Or it can mean exhausting something, as in "Finishing this glossary has worked my last nerve!"

Appendix Two

The Hankie Code

The hankie code is a relic of bygone days, back before gay culture had divided into so many subcultures. A hankie or bandanna (or several) was worn in the left or right back pocket to indicate what type of sex a man was interested in. It was particularly useful in noisy bars. The code seems to have fallen out of vogue, but friendly arguments as to what color means what still occur at cocktail parties.

Keys effectively replaced hankies with a simple, easy-to-remember code—left means top, right means bottom. If you want to know specifics, go say hello and find out. For a brief groovy moment in the early '90s, the wallet on a chain became the replacement for keys as code, but eventually both the right-handed and the left-handed decided that a wallet belonged on the convenient rather than the conveniently signaling side.

Legend says the hankie code started with the San Francisco 49ers (the miners, not the football team). At dances there were few if any women, so in order to do dances calling for male and female participants, half the fellows wore bandannas to signify that they were the girls (presumably on the right).

The code is elaborate, but the basics are as follows:

Navy blue
Signifies a desire for anal intercourse.

Red
Signifies a desire for fist fucking.

Black
Signifies a desire for heavy S/M.

Gray
Signifies a desire to engage in light S/M or bondage.

Yellow
Signifies a desire to engage in water sports.

Light blue
Signifies a desire to engage in oral sex.

Orange
Signifies a willingness to engage in absolutely anything.

Green
Signifies a hustler.